001
Early Ice Age couple with child

002
Ice Age cave dwellers

003
Ice Age couple building a fire

004
Later Ice Age men during a warm spell

005
Sumerian, 2500 B.C.

006
Sumerian couple at worship

007
Classic Sumerian dress

008
A couple from the late Sumerian period

009
Mesopotamian costume, eleventh century B.C.–569 B.C.

010
Assyrian soldiers and a camp follower

011
Assyrian queen and king, 668 B.C.

012
Babylonian king, ca. 550 B.C.
and Assyrian queen

013
Persian everyday wear

014
Persian merchant and woman

015
Persian woman, workingman, and religious man

016
Persian official, king, and attendant

017
Egypt, Old Kingdom; a king

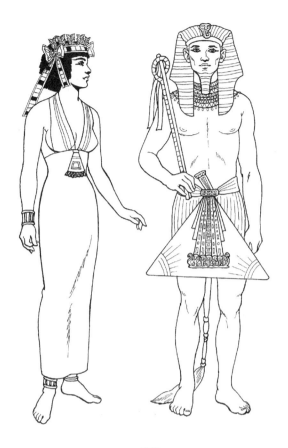

018
Egypt, Old Kingdom; a king and a woman

019
Egypt, Old Kingdom; a painter, or scribe, and his wife

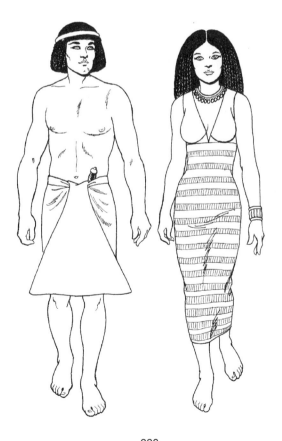

020
Egypt, Old Kingdom; a scribe and a woman

021
Egypt, Old Kingdom; a king and his wife

022
Egypt, Old Kingdom; an Egyptian couple of rank

023
Egypt, Middle Kingdom; a man and a woman

024
Egypt, Middle Kingdom; a king and a woman

025
Egypt, New Kingdom; a queen

026
Egypt, New Kingdom; a king

027
Egypt, New Kingdom; a king

028
Egypt, New Kingdom; a princess and a slave

029
Egypt, New Kingdom; a king

030
Egypt, New Kingdom; a queen

031
Egypt, New Kingdom; a pharaoh and a slave

032
Egypt, New Kingdom; a noble couple

033
Egypt, New Kingdom; a queen

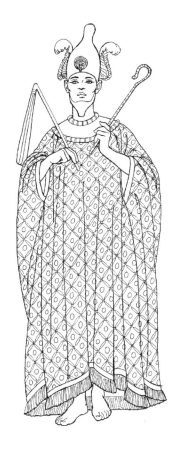

034
Egypt, New Kingdom; Osiris

035
Egypt, New Kingdom; a noblewoman and nobleman

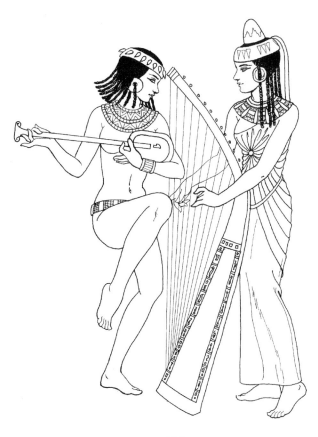

036
Egypt, New Kingdom; a slave and a musician

037
Egypt, New Kingdom; a woman

038
Egypt, New Kingdom; a soldier and a woman

039
Hair and headdress styles of ancient Egypt

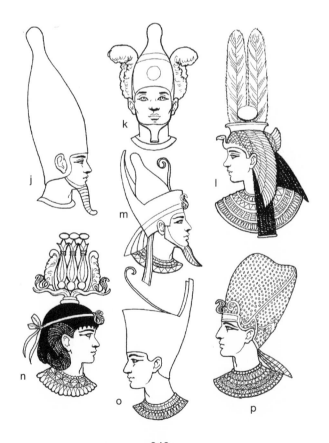

040
Hair and headdress styles of ancient Egypt

041
Cretan nobility, ca. 2000–1200 B.C.

042
Mycenaean common folk, ca. 1500–100 B.C.

043
Phrygian young woman and Amazon, ca. 1200–900 B.C.

044
The Greek chiton, ca. 500 B.C.

045
The Doric peplos

046
The Ionic chiton

047
The Greek chlamys, ca. 500 B.C.

048
Fashionable Greek women, ca. 600–480. B.C.

049
Greek warriors, ca. 440 B.C.

050
Greek rustic couple, ca. 480 B.C.

051
Banquet guest and dancing girl, ca. 500 B.C.

052
Greek serving girl and matron, ca. 250 B.C.

053
Etruscan couple, ca. 1000 B.C.

054
Etruscan couple, ca. 750 B.C.

055
Roman patricians, ca. 750 B.C.

056
Religious pilgrims, ca. 150 B.C.

057
Roman senator and woman, ca. 100–25 B.C.

058
Man and woman in everyday garb, ca. A.D. 25

059
Roman centurion and high officer, ca. A.D. 150–200

060
Germanic mercenary foot soldier and
Roman horseman, ca. A.D. 100–250

061
A Roman senator and his family, ca. A.D. 300–487

062
Gladiators and attendant, ca. A.D. 250–300

063
Grecian hairstyles and headgear, ca. 750–300 B.C.

064
Roman hairstyles and headgear, ca. 300–100 B.C.

065
Constantine and the angel (fourth century)

066
Fourth-century Byzantine woman and civil official

067
Fourth-century Christian commoners

068
Fourth-century Byzantine couple

069
Fourth-century royal couple

070
Emperor Arcadius and a warrior

071
Fourth-century Byzantine couple

072
Fifth-century Byzantine couple

073
Emperor Justinian and Empress Theodora

074
Empress Theodora

075
Galla Placida and Emperor Valentinian III

076
Sixth-century men of rank

077
Sixth-century noble couple

078
Seventh-century cavalryman and foot soldier

079
Seventh-century warrior and townswoman

080
Seventh-century courtier and priest

081
Emperor Romanus II and Empress Eudokia

082
Emperor Nicephorus III and his empress

083
Eleventh-century royal robes

084
Eleventh-century court dancer

Byzantine 21

085
Eleventh-century upper-class woman

086
Twelfth-century merchant and monk

087
Women's hairstyles of the Byzantine Empire

088
Men's hairstyles of the Byzantine Empire

089
Celtic-Norse couple, ca. 1000 B.C.

090
A Frankish family, ca. 800 B.C.

091
Teutonic couple, ca. 800 B.C.

092
Teutons, ca. 800 B.C.

093
Migrating nomadic tribe, ca. 400 B.C.

094
A European or Gallic farmer, ca. 300 B.C.

095
Migrating chieftain and warrior, ca. 400 B.C.

096
Gallic couple in a metalsmith's workshop, ca. 300 B.C.

097
British-Celtic warriors, ca. 150 B.C.

098
Gallic warriors, ca. 100 B.C.

099
Serfs, ca. 49 B.C.

100
Celtic Druids

101
Gallic warriors, ca. A.D. 100.

102
British warriors, ca. A.D. 500.

103
British women, ca. A.D. 600

104
British chieftain and soldier, A.D. 500.

105
Frankish warrior and woman

106
Charlemagne and a lady

107
Angles and Saxons, 10th century

108
Normans, 10th century

109
Ninth-century noblewomen

110
Tenth-century Frankish nobility

111
Eleventh-century soldier and knight

112
Eleventh-century peasants

113
Twelfth-century merchant and noblewoman

114
Twelfth-century Frankish royalty

115
Twelfth-century French commoners

116
Thirteenth-century knight and lady

117
Thirteenth-century nobility

118
Thirteenth-century German upper-class couple

119
Fourteenth-century French nobility

120
Fourteenth-century Flemish nobility

121
Fourteenth-century English princess and lady-in-waiting

122
Fourteenth-century English king and page

123
Fourteenth-century French nobleman

124
Fourteenth-century French noblewoman

125
Fifteenth-century English noblewoman

126
Fifteenth-century French nobility

127
Fourteenth-century Italian upper-class couple

128
Fourteenth-century Italian nobility

129
Fifteenth-century German nobility

130
Fifteenth-century German nobility

131
Fifteenth-century French peasants

132
Twelfth-century headdresses

133
Thirteenth-century headgear and coifs

134
Fourteenth-century headdresses

135
Fifteenth-century women's headgear

136
Fifteenth-century men's headgear

137
Italy, ca. 1400

138
Italy, Venetian man and woman, ca. 1400

139
Italy, Milanese couple, ca. 1410

140
Italy, ca. 1410

141
Germany and France, ca. 1420

142
Italy, ca. 1420

143
Italy, ca. 1430

144
Italy, ca. 1440

145
Italy, ca. 1440

146
Italy, ca. 1450

147
Italian couple, ca. 1460

148
Lady and minstrel, ca. 1490

149
Prosperous English family, ca. 1494

150
Italy, Venetian lady and dandy, ca. 1500

151
English noble and lady, ca. 1500

152
English country couple, ca. 1500

153
England, ca. 1500

154
Two English dandies, ca. 1500

155
English government officials, ca. 1504

156
Tudor gentleman and lady, ca. 1504

157
England, ca. 1510

158
Germany, ca. 1510

159
Germany, ca. 1510

160
France, ca. 1510

161
Katherine of Aragon, ca. 1510

162
English ladies of the court, ca. 1528

163
Italy, ca. 1530

164
Italian courtesans bleaching and styling their hair, ca. 1530

165
France, ca. 1530

166
France, ca. 1530

167
Henry VIII of England, ca. 1534

168
Anne Boleyn, ca. 1534

42   Renaissance and Tudor

169
Jane Seymour, ca. 1536

170
Anne of Cleves, ca. 1539

171
French court couple, ca. 1540

172
Italian courtesan, ca. 1540

Renaissance and Tudor   43

173
Catherine Howard, ca. 1540

174
Princess Elizabeth, ca. 1546

175
German royal children with their nanny, ca. 1550

176
French courtiers wearing Spanish-style attire, ca. 1550

177
Upper-class French merchant and his wife, ca. 1550

178
London merchant family, ca. 1550–1560

179
Prince Edward VI and attendant, ca. 1550

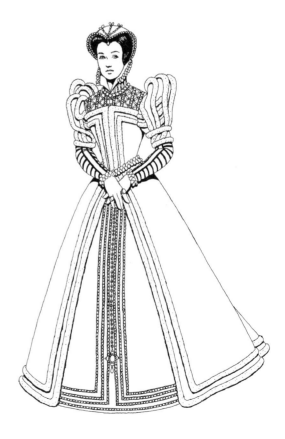

180
Mary Tudor, ca. 1552

181
Mary Tudor and Philip of Spain, ca. 1554

182
Members of the Elizabethan court, ca. 1558–1560

183
Mary of Scotland and Lord Darnley, ca. 1566

184
Elizabethan lady and her husband, ca. 1580

185
Elizabeth I of England, ca. 1588

186
Two London ladies of high rank, ca. 1590

187
English sailor and farmer, ca. 1600

188
English nobleman and lady, ca. 1600

189
Women's headgear and hairstyles,1400–1450

190
Men's headgear and hairstyles, 1400–1450

191
Men's headgear and hairstyles, 1450–1490

192
Men's headgear and hairstyles, 1500–1550

193
Women's headgear and hairstyles, 1450–1500

194
Hats, shoes, and accessories, 1490–1640

195
Hats, shoes, and accessories, 1500–1600

196
Women's headgear and hairstyles, 1500–1550

197
Greek and Roman footwear

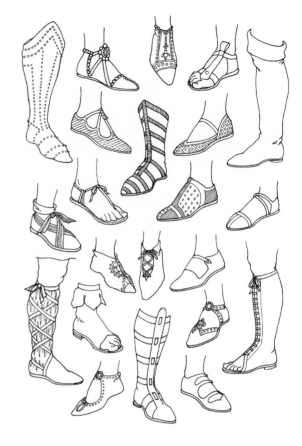

198
Byzantine footwear

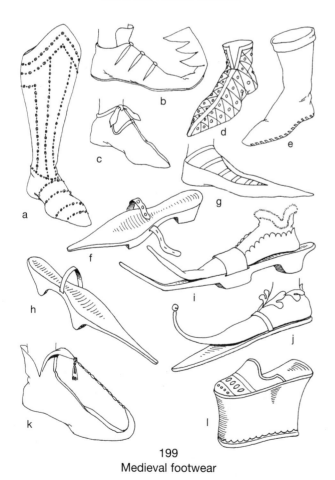

199
Medieval footwear

200
Renaissance footwear and accessories

A SHORT HISTORY OF COSTUME

PREHISTORIC

The great ancient civilizations developed in the valleys of the Euphrates, Nile, and Indus rivers, tropical areas where exposure to the blazing sun may have prompted early man to develop a portable shade in the form of capes and head coverings. In the succession of Ice Ages in Northern Europe, protection from cold was probably the primary motivation for the development of clothing.

Prehistoric man in glacial areas survived by hunting. Very likely, he soon learned that animals were useful for their pelts as well as their flesh. At first, the hides were probably used as a means of camouflage; draped over the body, with the head still attached, so that the hunter could move closer to his prey. The hunter learned that the hide covering gave him warmth as well as invisibility. It probably took centuries for primitive Ice Age peoples to learn to soften dried hides so that they could be shaped to move with the body. Chewing the hide was probably the first method used. Later, oiling the skin became a temporary means of softening skins. Finally ancient man discovered the process of tanning, a technique of soaking the skins in a solution of water containing tannic acid from the barks of oak and willow trees. Once man had learned to make hides soft, the next challenge was to shape them. The development of the eyed needle was a great technological advance. Bone and ivory needles have been found in Paleolithic caves, dating to more than forty thousand years ago.

Meanwhile, peoples of the more temperate farming climates were learning how to use animal and vegetable fibers for fabrics. The ancestors of the Mongols of Central Asia discovered that they could wet sheep and goat wool, roll it tightly in a leather mat, beat it with sticks or paddles, and let it dry. The felt thus produced was durable and pliable, and could be cut into shapes for garments, rugs, tents, etc. Bark cloth was produced by soaking the barks or stems of certain trees and plants, layering them crosswise, pounding them until they matted together, then drying them in sheets which were then oiled to give more flexibility. Bark cloth was not easily cut or sewn, so was usually used for capes or wraparound garments.

Once mankind settled down and began farming, weaving developed. Only then could crops such as flax, hemp, and cotton be cultivated and turned into fine, flexible fibers.

MESOPOTAMIAN

Perhaps the world's first non-nomadic civilization was that developed in ancient Mesopotamia (an area roughly covered by present-day Iraq), a land watered and kept fertile by two great rivers, the Tigris and the Euphrates. One of the first flourishing cultures was the Sumerian, which dates from about 3500 to 2370 B.C. Early Sumerian dress consisted of a simple sheepskin kilt wrapped around the loins and held in place by a metal pin. Often another piece of sheepskin was thrown over the shoulder like a cape. The skins were worn hide side in with the wool twisted into a pattern of points called kaunakes. As the civilization developed, felted fabrics, then woven fabrics, were employed. Our only records of Sumerian clothing are from highly stylized sculptures and mosaics. Both men and women are generally shown barefooted, the men's heads are shaved, and the women wear their hair in a chignon or roll, usually held in place with bands of jewelry. Long cloaks were also worn, often with the edges cut into scalloped or dagged edges. Men wore leather and metal helmets. Poor people and priests went naked, although priests generally wore a belt or girdle to signify their position. The Sumerians showed great skill in working with metal, especially gold. They used lapis lazuli, carnelian, and other semiprecious stones to enhance their jewelry.

Mesopotamia's history was one of conquest and reconquest by the Akkadians, Assyrians, Babylonians, and others. With the influence of these Semitic peoples, and with a later revival of Sumerian culture between about 2370 and 2000 B.C., Mesopotamian costume altered and became more varied. A draped style replaced the sheepskin skirt. Both sexes wore a long, rectangular shawl that was fringed on the edge and was wrapped around the body in a spiral. The men generally left the left arm and shoulder free for more mobility, while the women generally covered their arms with sleeves from an under-tunic. It was fashionable for men to grow their hair and beard long and even to curl it, arranging it in corkscrew curls at the ends. Women wore their hair even longer, and also curled and even frizzed it. Both men and women used false hair when needed. The final stage of dress for the people of Mesopotamia was roughly from the eleventh century B.C. to 539 B.C. when Babylon fell to the Persians. The basic garments for both Babylonians and Assyrians were the tunic and the shawl, with men wearing a short-sleeved tunic, women a long. The tunic could range from knee to ankle length, and shawls could be either rectangular or semi-circular. Underwear for men consisted of a loincloth, for women a short skirt (these garments were also what the poor and common laborers wore as outerwear). Men's apparel was more elaborately and richly decorated than women's. Wool and linen garments were brightly dyed and embroidered in colored wool or golden thread. Footwear was of brightly dyed leather. There was a wide range of headwear from a simple felt fez-like cap to jeweled fillets to tall truncated cone crowns.

PERSIAN EMPIRE

The Persian Empire replaced the Assyro-Babylonian empires in the sixth century B.C. Persian dress was developed by nomadic tribes of horsemen. For everyday wear both Persian men and women wore trousers. The Persian man's basic costume was a knee-length tunic, belted at the waist, with long set-in sleeves, worn over wide-topped trousers with tapering legs that were gathered to fit tightly at the ankle. Boots or high-topped shoes were worn. A long coat was often worn. Early Persian women generally wore a long tunic over trousers and a wrapped head covering. The Persians soon adopted the ceremonial robes and hairstyles of the peoples they had conquered. Robes similar to those of the Assyrians became the ceremonial and royal styles, although trousers were still worn underneath. Women adopted plainer versions of earlier Assyrian styles, including the ankle-length dress with an underskirt, a shawl draped around the body, and a head veil that covered the mouth. After Alexander the Great conquered Persia, the draped Greek mode was adopted, and prevailed until the third century A.D., when there was a revival of traditional Persian trousers and long tunics.

Although their roots go back as far as the Sumerians, Hebrew styles seem to have codified during the Persian Empire. Jewish culture seemed not to have adopted Persian trousers, preferring to stay with the traditional tunic.

ANCIENT EGYPTIAN

Ancient Egypt was established about 3100 B.C., a result of the union of upper Egypt (the Nile Valley) and lower Egypt (the Nile Delta). Its history has been divided into three important eras, separated by periods of turmoil: the Old Kingdom (ca. 2686 B.C.), the age of pyramid building; the Middle Kingdom (ca. 2040–1786 B.C.), the period of power and growth; and the New Kingdom (ca. 1570–1085 B.C.), which began in magnificence and ended with Roman conquest.

Over the course of three thousand years, ancient Egyptian fashions changed only imperceptibly. People wore draped, sheer garments—loincloths, skirts, capes, and robes—fastened with knots, belts, or sashes.

Clothing in the Old Kingdom was notable for its simplicity. Men wore kilt-like skirts called schenti, which evolved from loincloths. Variations on this style depended on the wearer's rank, as well as the occasion.

Women wore a tightly wrapped sheath called a kalasiris. Falling from below the breast to the ankle, it was held up by one or two straps. Eventually, kalasiris came to describe any seamed, dress-like piece of clothing worn by men or women.

In ancient Egypt, nudity was a natural state. Laborers and slaves, if clothed, wore only loincloths. For a slave, often the sole covering was a cloth belt inscribed with his or her master's name. Children living in the early dynasties were also unclothed. Clothing was a status symbol, but cleanliness was more important.

To keep clean, men and women shaved their bodies, including their heads. They wore wigs, which could be washed or replaced, to protect their scalps from the sun. Wigs, which appear to have been made from rolled strips of cornhusks, were often braided. Beards were considered symbols of power, so pharaohs wore false wooden beards that were held in place by chin straps.

During the Middle Kingdom, jewelry became more refined and brightly colored. Crafted in gold, it was often set with semiprecious stones, including lapis lazuli and garnets.

With the influence of outside cultures, New Kingdom clothing became layered and more varied. Pleated and gathered fabrics in rich primary colors were popular, although diaphanous robes and gowns were usually white.

By the time of the New Kingdom, men had discarded the schenti in favor of skirts made from linen rectangles folded into single box pleats at the front. The nobility wore skirts made from more generous amounts of fabric that fanned into wide, single triangles in the front. They were fastened with decorative belts. Hanging from each skirt was a wedge-shaped apron, elaborately embroidered, and adorned with precious stones. The front-piece, without the decoration, was adapted by the lower classes.

Another style introduced during the New Kingdom was a sleeved tunic that resembled a short-sleeved nightshirt. The most unusual garment of this period was made from a rectangle of fabric about twice the height of the wearer. It was folded down the center and had a slit cut for the head. The sides, sewn from hem to waist, were caught up and tied in the front, creating voluminous sleeves. Inspired by a style from Asia Minor, it was worn in ancient Egypt by both men and women.

Throughout Egypt's ancient history, most people, including royalty, went barefoot. During the New Kingdom period, however, people of rank began to wear papyrus and palm leaf sandals for ceremonies. Nobles wore gloves.

GREEK AND ROMAN

Our information about ancient Crete (ca. 2000–1500 B.C.) is limited to fragments of murals and some carvings and ceramics. Clothing designs were quite elegant and indicate skill in sewing and dressmaking, with pleating, set-in sleeves, layering, and embroidery. The Cretans' imaginative jewelry shows great technical knowledge.

Among the people of Asia Minor who were precursors of classical Greek civilization were the Phrygians. Both sexes wore sewn garments with narrow, fitted sleeves and fitted leggings or hose (probably knitted). Garments often were delicately patterned (probably embroidered). Phrygian use of the draped scarf was ancestral to the classic Greek and Roman choice of garments that were draped, tied, and pinned.

Three items were basic to classic Greek dress: the chiton, a linen shirtlike garment; the peplos, an overgarment worn only by women; and the chlamys, a cloak. These three garments were draped and girdled to create varied styles. Greek fashions from ca. 600 B.C. still showed many earlier influences, such as patterned fabrics and elaborately braided borders. By 500 B.C. the chiton was made of two long rectangles of fabric, of a width from elbow to elbow. The sides were stitched together for two-thirds of the length and the top opening was pinned to form two shoulder straps. Females often wore two girdles, or waistbands, with the fabric pouched over them. Men wore a single girdle at the waist. The chlamys now was a male garment. Women's cloaks (the himation), also rectangular, were much longer. Later, both sexes wore the himation over the chiton, and men wore it, with no other garment, for formal and state occasions. The common men and women usually wore only the short chiton.

North of what was to become Rome was the ancient country of Etruria. The Etruscan cloak, the tabenna, was semicircular. The Etruscans also wore a tunic similar to the Greek chiton. Etruscan women's robes, sewn with a fitted bodice and flared skirt, were worn with a short jacket or a cloak.

Probably early Roman dress for men was a shirtlike tunica and a cloak, the toga. The toga, uniquely Roman, was similar in drape and use to the Greek chlamys, but was semicircular and very long, with the width twice the length. The part of the toga that went over the left shoulder was pulled up and bloused in the front, forming a pocket. Another type of Roman cloak, the paenula, was bell-shaped, sewn down the sides, and often worn with a hood. The tunica was sewn down both sides and usually had short sleeves. It was cut wide and girdled, just like the Greek chiton. To go outdoors dressed only in a tunica was considered bad form, except for workmen. A longer tunica (tunica manicata) did not become popular until about A.D. 300. Many men wore only the toga. On the tunica were worn badges of rank in the form of colored bands or braid, called clavi. For example, senators wore wide purple stripes called laticlavia and victorious generals wore golden embroidered palm-leaf stripes called palmata. The wearing of any kind of hose was forbidden by law in the city of Rome. However, as the empire waned, the military adopted breeches such as those the Gauls and Persians wore—probably inspired by the chill of Britain and of desert nights.

The principal items of dress for Roman women were a shirt or chemise (tunica intima), a dress over it, and a cloaklike garment. The woman's tunica was similar in cut to the man's, but reached the floor. Often it was of light wool, but in later centuries sheer fabrics were used. Usually it was adorned at the shoulders with clasps or buttons. Most Roman women girdled the tunica under the breasts. Over this was worn a stola, cut exactly like the tunica, but with full sleeves. Its draping was considered an art form, and it often was adorned with colorful braids, pearls, and spangles. The third garment, the palla, was worn outside the house. At first the palla resembled the male toga, but later it became more voluminous and rectangular. On the street the women wore a veil called a flammeum, which was attached to the back of the hair and extended down the back.

Roman males usually pulled their togas over their heads when the weather was bad. Travelers sometimes wore hats of felt or braided straw. Laborers, sailors, and hunters often wore caps of leather or straw. At the height of the Roman Empire women's hairstyles became extremely elaborate and varied. Footwear was an important feature of Roman dress. Women's shoe styles were similar to men's but were more elegantly decorated with gold braids, pearls, and jewels.

The abundant traces of color left on unearthed statuary show that ancient Greek costume was very colorful, as was Roman garb. Gold trims, jewels, and spangles decorated their fabrics, and beautifully made jewelry was worn.

BYZANTINE

The Byzantine Empire began in A.D. 330, when Emperor Constantine I moved the capital of the Roman Empire to Byzantium. In A.D. 364, Emperor Valentinian I divided the Roman Empire into two parts—east and west—with two emperors, to facilitate the management of the vast territory. After the fall of Rome in the fifth century, the eastern Byzantine Empire ruled alone. This empire lasted for over 1,100 years—until 1453, the year of the death of Emperor Constantine XI and the fall of the empire to the Ottoman Turks.

During this era, costume attained a richness of color, fabric, and ornament that far exceeded the greatest days of Rome. The Byzantine Empire's thriving trade led to immense wealth. The Byzantine culture was a complex blending of east and west. Included within Byzantine fashions are not only those styles worn in the city of Byzantium after it became the capital of the Roman Empire, but also clothing worn in regions that fell under its influence, such as Italy, Greece, and Russia. Until the sixth century, the Roman influence was still strong, with draped styles predominating. The tunica, the dalmatic (a wide-sleeved over-robe of cotton, linen, or wool for the commoners, and silk for the wealthy), and the stola were the basic foundations of Byzantine style. The dalmatic evolved from knee-length in the early part of the empire (sixth to tenth centuries) to floor-length (tenth to thirteenth centuries), finally resembling a Turkish caftan in the fourteenth and fifteenth centuries. From the beginning, the fabrics and colors used were strongly influenced by Persian, Assyrian, Egyptian, and Arabian sources. As time passed, these eastern styles of costume began to assert themselves in the form of trousers, footwear, head coverings and, above all, decoration and jewelry.

Most of our knowledge of Byzantine fashions comes from surviving mosaics and sculptures. Clothing artifacts reveal remarkably intricate, elaborate brocaded fabrics with jeweled surfaces. These brocaded fabrics gave a new stiffness and luminosity to garments. The Emperor Justinian introduced the manufacture of silk to Constantinople in the sixth century. Silk fabric allowed for the use of brilliant colors. A uniquely Byzantine article worn at court was the tablion (sometimes called a clavus), an ornamental, jewel-encrusted, rectangular piece of fabric inset on men's and women's cloaks. The tablion identified the wearer as a member of the royal house or a court dignitary. Another unusual garment was the Persian-derived maniakis, a separate collar of gold-embroidered, jewel-encrusted fabric.

Byzantine dress typically covered the arms and legs. After the eighth century, the lorum was introduced—a long scarf that was draped around the body. The lorum was generally made of silk or gold cloth and was heavily jeweled, indicating the wearer's status. Men of means draped themselves in a rich dalmatic with a tablion placed on the left front edge. Women wore a stola over their long tunicas, using one end of the garment as a head covering. Both men and women fastened their mantles on the right shoulder with an ornate jeweled clasp called a fibula. The camisia, an undergarment made of linen or silk, was worn beneath the tunica. The long tunica evolved into the gunna (gown). In the latter centuries of Byzantine rule, a short shirt with long dolman-style sleeves, called a juppe, was worn over long tunicas.

Elaborately designed jewelry was a hallmark of the Byzantine era. Pearls were plentiful and used lavishly with diamonds and other precious gems; eventually, colored glass beads and tiny mirrors were added to decorative embroideries. Women enveloped their hair in a coif of silk or net worked with pearls. Sandals, standard footwear in Roman days, were still worn, but soft ankle-high boots called calcei were the preferred footwear of the wealthy. The boots were generally made of soft, brightly colored leather, often embroidered and jeweled, and had long, pointed toes.

The Byzantine Empire made two important contributions to western fashion. In the third century, its weavers began using shuttles to produce patterned fabrics. Later, in the sixth century, Emperor Justinian initiated the raising of silkworms from the cocoon. Under his aegis, silkworm eggs and seeds of the mulberry bush, concealed in hollow bamboo staffs, were brought into Byzantium by two Persian monks. The Byzantine mode of dressing became more and more sumptuous until the fall of the empire; its influence is evident throughout the Medieval and Renaissance periods of European fashion. In addition, it provided the foundation for the liturgical costume of both the eastern and western Christian churches, particularly those of Russia.

NORTHERN EUROPEAN

Before there was recorded history, there is archaeological evidence that a tribe (or tribes) of nomads from the north plains of the central Indian continent wandered into Europe. These people were the forebearers of the Celts, and over the following centuries their descendants mingled with local peoples, forming new tribes and nationalities throughout north Europe.

Centuries before the Roman Empire appeared, the Northern European "barbarians," most of whom shared Celtic ancestry, were trading with Etruscans and Greeks. They created the first art style in mainland Europe as well as introducing iron and bronze technology. Metal workers from the northern tribes were noted for their craftsmanship and artistry. The most consistent design elements throughout the history of Celtic and Barbarian art are intertwined and elaborate geometric shapes found in many of the earliest archaeological sites, the earliest known being the double-spiraled motif found on stone carvings to jewelry.

As the barbarians became more technologically proficient, there evolved a ruling class in the form of tribal chieftains. They were never able to unify into a single powerful nation or empire as did the Romans. Many of the barbarian women enjoyed equal rights with their men, continuing to own their own property after marriage, and they often fought alongside the men in battle, with some ruling as chieftains of their tribes.

By 400 B.C. Celtic leaders were generally being selected by vote rather than by inheritance. By the first century B.C. the Gallic-Celts were being subjugated and Romanized by the Roman military machine to the south. The Gallic-Celtic language was Romanized to become French. Only in Ireland would a Celtic culture remain intact, surviving long after the Roman Empire had fallen.

During the sixth to eighth centuries, Celtic Ireland assumed an important role in the spread of Christianity, carrying it to Wales, Britain, France, North Italy, Austria, Germany, and Switzerland.

By the time of Roman domination in the first century B.C. and A.D., there was little difference in the dress of the Gauls and the Irish-Celts. Both men and women wore belted tunics and cloaks fastened by a fibula. Cloaks could be especially fancy and colorful, frequently indicating social status, and tunics could be of many colors. Brightly colored hooded Celtic cloaks became internationally popular among the rich, especially in Rome. By the fifth century A.D. Rome had fallen to the Goths and was no longer a force in England or Ireland. As the Romans withdrew, the English isles were invaded by Germanic tribes (principally the Saxons, the Angles, and the Jutes). Many of the Romanized Celts fled to Wales, Cornwall, or Brittany to form the "Celtic Fringe," which lasts to the present.

In the eighth and ninth centuries A.D., the Vikings repeatedly invaded Anglo-Saxon England and Celtic Ireland, plundering and killing for many years. Eventually the plunderers settled in and became assimilated with the Irish-Celts, English, and even Scots. The last invasion of the English Isles came in the eleventh century from Normandy and William the Conqueror.

MEDIEVAL

The medieval era, or Middle Ages, is defined by historians as the period in western European history between the fall of Rome in the fifth century and the rise of the Renaissance in the mid-fifteenth century. Overall, fashions during this time continued to reflect the influences of the Greek, Roman, and Byzantine cultures.

Most historians reckon the beginning of the Middle Ages with the ascension to power of Charlemagne, King of the Franks, in 768. He united by conquest nearly all Christian lands of western Europe and ruled as emperor from 800 to 814. He had a close alliance with Rome, and the Byzantine influence in fashion was apparent in his court, though in a less splendid style.

With the rise of the feudal system in the late 800s, style and extravagance of dress became a reflection of one's position in society. By the late 1400s, the cost of clothing and the lengths of items such as hoods, trains, and shoes were regulated by sumptuary laws that remained in effect until the early sixteenth century.

Among the earliest articles of clothing from this time was a tunic with long sleeves called a bliaud. It was worn knee length by men and floor length by women. By the eleventh century, men wore the bliaud lengthened to the ankle. At the end of the thirteenth century, the bliaud, then called a tunic, was worn by young men a mere few inches below the waist.

The bliaud covered a chainse, or under-tunic, usually colored saffron yellow. Originally made of heavy wool, linen, or hemp, the chainse eventually evolved into a piece of lingerie made of sheer, washable fabric. Another garment worn by men and women was the mantle, a luxuriant cloak fastened in front by a large brooch, buckle, or pin.

Increased trade with the Orient and Far East brought new dyes to Europe that were used to produce fabrics in brilliant shades of scarlet, green, blue, and purple. While materials tended to be rich and heavy, embroidered, or fur trimmed, delicate linens, embroideries, velvets, and sheer gauzes became available.

In the thirteenth century the surcoat replaced the bliaud. Based on the sleeveless cloth covering worn over armor by knights to fend off the glare of the sun, the surcoat was adopted by both men and women. The woman's surcoat was open at the sides to reveal a fitted dress with long buttoned sleeves called a cote-hardie. Men wore the cote-hardie too, cut shorter. Both men and women wore jeweled hip girdles, or belts.

In the fourteenth century, parti-colored clothes became the rage. Garments were divided into halves or quarters, each section sewn from a contrasting color. Shoes and stockings were different colors as well.

By the fifteenth century, the surcoat began to disappear. Women wore a belted dress called a robe that had a long-sleeved, fitted bodice joined to a full skirt. Men wore jackets that covered a quilted garment, with or without sleeves, called a pourpoint.

For outerwear, women wore flowing capes that were lined with fur in winter. A popular men's cloak was the houppelande, a trailing robe with long bishop's sleeves, fastened in folds at the waist by a jeweled belt.

Dagged edges, a petal-like scalloping, were popular decoration for all parts of clothing. Small silver bells, favored ornaments for men and women, appeared on belts, girdles, sashes, hats, and the toes of shoes.

Head coverings for men included skullcaps, helmets, peaked bonnets, and hats with rolled brims. Crusaders sometimes wore straw hats over their metal helmets to deflect the sun. By the eleventh century, soft fabric caps with peaked tops were in general use. Men also wore toques or bag caps. Sugarloaf-shaped hats made of felt were worn with and without brims. Feathers as hat ornaments first appeared in the medieval era; the peacock plume was most popular.

By the twelfth century, the chaperon, a hooded cape, became the most common headgear for men. While the hood remained in fashion through the sixteenth century, with only nobles allowed to wear long hoods, during the fourteenth century the peak of the hood lengthened into a liripipe. A streamer of gauze or ribbon that sometimes reached the floor, the liripipe was also restricted to use by nobility. Stuffed turbans, called roundlets, were trimmed with liripipes, too.

During the Middle Ages, the Christian church required that women cover their heads. The predominant head covering for women was a square, oblong, or round piece of fabric called a couvre-chef, wimple, or headrail. In earlier centuries, the basic headrail was wrapped around a woman's neck and shoulders, held in place by a circlet or crown. Beginning in the twelfth century, the wimple became a longer length of fabric, usually white linen, that was drawn up under a woman's chin and fastened on top of her head. Over the wimple, women wore a separate couvre-chef that was held in place by a crown or circlet. In the twelfth century, blonde hair was fashionable. Some women sat for hours on enclosed terraces waiting for the sun to bleach their tresses. Others

used false hair and cosmetics. During the thirteenth century women began to wear small, crownlike toques, a headband, and chin-band, all in white linen. In the fourteenth century the caul came into fashion. This style concealed a woman's hair in a silken case covered with a heavy net of jeweled silver or gold cord. Hair coverings varied widely, from a simple snoodlike net to cylindrical cauls worn on either side of the face, to a padded horn or heart-shaped headdress fastened over the caul. Women often wore sheer veils on top of the entire combination. They plucked the visible hair at the napes of their necks, at their temples, and thinned their eyebrows.

In the fourteenth century, the hennin, or steeple headdress, was introduced. A tall cone, the hennin had a black velvet band across the top of the forehead. Always draped with a floating or wired veil, the height of the hennin became so extravagant that the authorities imposed regulations here, too. The higher the hennin, the more exalted a person's place in society.

The chin-band, a folded white linen wrapped under a woman's chin, fastening to a band around her forehead, came into style during the fifteenth century. In another style of head covering, a stiffened headband was shaped into a low toque or crownlike headdress.

Men and women wore similar soft leather or fabric shoes with elongated toes. These low-cut shoes buttoned or tied at the ankle. One men's style, the poulaine, had pointed toes that became so long that they had to be stuffed to hold their shapes. Eventually the exaggerated toes were held up by fine chains attached to the knees. Also called a poulaine was a clog or patten made of wood that was worn to protect the soft soles of shoes.

Men wore fitted and sewn stockings or tights. Made of bias-cut material, they were decorated with jeweled garters. Stockings, held up at the waist with a belt or tie, were cross-gartered on the lower leg with bands of fabric or soft leather.

Heavy chains and jeweled belts were popular accessories among wealthy people, who used them to carry pouches, purses, and daggers set with precious stones.

RENAISSANCE

The Renaissance period, which began around the year 1400 in Italy, continued through the 1500s. During that time, Europe made the transition from the plague-ridden medieval world into a more modern and affluent era.

Renaissance fashions at first retained many medieval features. Women still wore wimples, hennins with elaborate veils, and houppelandes over chemises. Men still wore houppelandes over short jackets and long, often multicolor hose, and sported long, pointed shoes and fancy turbans.

Italy's shipowners and merchants brought gorgeous silks and brocades, new dyestuffs, and previously unseen jewelry, perfumes, and spices to Europe from East Asia. As trade expanded, an affluent middle class developed. Italian fashions were comparatively simple and lightweight, emphasizing luxurious fabrics, elegant jewelry, and brilliant colors. Men wore a tight-fitting basic outfit: hose; a white or colored shirt made of linen, silk, or taffeta; and a waist-long jacket called a doublet, or a hip-length one called a jerkin. The "codpiece" was designed as a practical covering for the frontal opening in men's tights. This triangular flap, tied in place, soon became an often blatantly sexual embellishment to a man's garb. It also was useful for storage of small, valuable possessions.

By 1450 the separate bodice, skirt, and sleeves were in vogue. The elaborate sleeves were made of contrasting rich materials, jeweled, and hugely puffed, or they were slashed, with puffs of the undergarment or chemise pulled through. The tight, boned bodice was the costume's foundation.

As trade carried Italian fashions north into the colder climates of France, Germany, and England, quilted linings, padded with wool or with straw, were added to garments for warmth. This padding made men's bodies look tanklike on spindly, tight-clad shanks, and gave women a bulky, covered-up silhouette. Generally, English costume was less graceful than the Italian, but less overblown than the German.

During the 1500s, the wealthy traveled throughout western Europe; one country's fashions were adapted in others. German costume was elaborately decorated with slashing, ribbons, and embroidery. By 1550 the English, French, and Spanish courts used German styles, toned down a bit. A Continental style was found in all countries. England and Spain by then were vying for domination of oceanic trade, supplanting Italy; they also dislodged Italy from fashion leadership. The "Spanish style" for women, with its confining boiled-leather corset and conical farthingale (a hooped-framework underskirt) under elaborate petticoats, became fashionable throughout Europe.

In England, the Renaissance corresponds to the Tudor and Elizabethan periods, so named after the British monarchs at the time. The monarchs of the English Tudor and Elizabethan dynasties were Henry VII (1485–1509), Henry VIII (1509–1547), Edward VI (1547–1553), Mary (1553–1558), and Elizabeth I (1558–1603). During the early Tudor period, the Italian Renaissance was in full swing, and fashion innovations found their way to the newly prosperous middle class in England. By the end of Henry VII's reign, the men's costume consisted of a jerkin, worn over a waistcoat. The codpiece was worn over the front of men's breeches. Bobbed hair with bangs was the most popular men's style. The bell-shaped canvas underskirt—forerunner to the hoop—was a new fashion item for women.

Henry VIII, who inherited a highly prosperous kingdom from his father, enacted sumptuary laws whose purpose was to distinguish between the social classes by their dress. The Tudor gentleman of the 1530s wore linen shirts and full-length hose fastened to a belt or a doublet. A surcoat was worn over the doublet. The shovel-shaped "lion's paw" shoe was worn by both men and women. Men's hair was cropped short; mustaches and beards were common. Women's clothing styles had changed little from the previous years—velvet gowns worn with stiff brocaded silk petticoats, low-cut squared yokes, and headdresses still prevailed.

During the reigns of Edward VI and Mary Tudor, clothing was less ornate, and less jewelry was worn. "French hoods" (caps stiffened with wire) and velvet bonnets completed the costumes. The ruff marked this period—women wore large ruffled cambric collars, often edged with lace, in cartwheel or fan shapes, wired and starched to great lengths and heights. Women's hair, tightly curled and waved, was arranged high on a jeweled frame.

From the early 1500s corsets were worn, made at first of rigid hinged iron, and later on of flexible steel bands. By Elizabeth's time they were shaped by boned fabric. Corsets were adopted by men who wanted to acquire the narrower male silhouette. Hair dye and cosmetics were widely used by stylish women. In the late 1550s, the drum farthingale—a huge, circular hip-level hoop introduced from France—became the skirt of choice. The hoop made sitting in a chair virtually impossible, so the wearers lounged on cushions piled on the floor. Neck and sleeve ruffs came in sets and were delivered in a "band box." Men, as well as women, wore ornate jewelry and pearls, men favoring a single drop-shaped pearl earring. Tall hats, made of velvet, felt, or beaver, were worn by both the merchant class and nobility.

The advent of the printing press in the mid-fifteenth century helped spread information about style and fashion, and the English delighted in each style change emanating from Europe, especially Italy. They adapted these fashions to their own taste, creating truly distinctive Tudor and Elizabethan styles.

ABOUT THE ILLUSTRATIONS

001. Early Ice Age couple with child. This couple is wearing draped furs, possibly pinned with a sharpened bone. The man has wrapped leggings of softer skins, such as rabbit, held in place by leather strips.

002. Ice Age cave dwellers. The men have brought home their kill for the women to butcher and clean the hides. The cape and the wraparound skirt were probably the earliest garments.

003. Ice Age couple building a fire. The woman wears a tanned leather skirt, while the man wears a cape, tied at the waist with a leather thong. He is using moss to kindle a fire. Ice Age people also used moss to stuff into their clothing for extra insulation.

004. Later Ice Age men during a warm spell. The man on the left is wearing a loin cloth and leggings, both made of tanned leather, while the man on the right is wearing a hide loincloth, fur side in, and a leather arrow pouch hanging from his thong waistband.

005. Sumerian, 2500 B.C. The man on the left, an army official, wears a leather helmet, a felt cloak, and a felt tunic with a scalloped edge in the style of the kaunakes. A Sumerian king stands on the right wearing a small felt shoulder cloak and a sheepskin kaunakes. On his head is a beaten gold helmet that imitates a stylized ceremonial hairdo with a sculptured fillet and topknot.

006. Sumerian couple at worship. This couple is presenting a food offering to the gods. A priest, wearing only a girdle, carries an offering into the temple. The man is of the later Sumerian period. He is wearing a beard in the style of the Semitic peoples who took over and greatly influenced Sumerian culture, but wears the traditional Sumerian scalloped skirt. The woman is wearing a late Sumerian saronglike gown that hangs from one shoulder and opens via a crossover flap over the left breast. Her hair is worn in a roll held by a fillet of ribbon. The dress could be of a single color, or as here, two colors of fabric.

007. Classic Sumerian dress. The woman wears a dress of felted wool with loops of fabric applied in the kaunakes pattern. On her head she wears a gold headdress of leaves and flowers. The man wears a wool kaunakes gown with a fringed shoulder cloak.

008. A couple from the late Sumerian period. She wears her hair in a frizzed style with a gold headband across the forehead, and her dress is in the Semitic style. The man is playing a lyre and wears a felt scalloped skirt with a waistband looped to the side. His hairdo is of the Semitic style, although he is beardless.

009. Mesopotamian costume, eleventh century B.C.–569 B.C. The costume of the peoples of Mesopotamia had fully evolved by the eleventh century B.C., and changed little through the fall of the Babylonian Empire. The man on the left wears an older-styled Sumerian mantle with a lambskin cap. The woman wears a basic long-sleeved tunic with a felt cap and a jeweled collar at her neck, while the man on the right wears the basic short-sleeved tunic of the period.

010. Assyrian soldiers and a camp follower. Left, an Assyrian warrior with a helmet and a broad girdle over a short-sleeved tunic; he is carrying a lance and shield. Center, an armored archer, and right, a woman camp follower in a basic tunic and fringed mantle.

011. Assyrian queen and king, 668 B.C. The queen wears a richly decorated tunic with tight, highly ornamented sleeves, under a fringed and embroidered under-mantle, with a fringed, solid color over-mantle. The king wears a high felt cap with gold braid whose ends fall down the back. His short-sleeved tunic is fringed in gold and wraps around the body. He wears a gold-fringed mantle over one shoulder and gold bracelets on his upper arm and wrists, as well as gold earrings. His sword is worn in the horizontal position of the Assyrian warrior.

012. Babylonian king, ca. 550 B.C., and Assyrian queen. He wears a high molded felt cap topped by a jeweled ornament, with gold braid ribbons hanging down the back. His tunic and mantle are of contrasting colored fabrics and are elaborately embroidered in gold thread and heavily fringed. His shoes are of gold embroidered soft leather. The queen wears matching tunic and mantle, both elaborately embroidered in gold and fringed.

013. Persian everyday wear. The man on the left wears a knee-length belted tunic over trousers with boots, topped by a long coat with set-in sleeves. The coat has ties at the chest. He wears a molded felt cap. The woman wears a long tunic, girdled at the waist, over trousers and buttoned shoes. The warrior on the right wears a long-sleeved shirt under a knee-length tunic with long slotted sleeves. He wears a felt cap and carries lances and a shield.

014. Persian merchant and woman. A merchant of standing wears a long coat, elaborately trimmed with embroidery of red and gold thread, over a long tunic and trousers. He has buttoned shoes of soft leather and wears a Phrygian-styled cap decorated with an embroidered band. The woman is dressed in the later style of dress with a long tunic, a shawl, and a head covering. At her neck she wears jewelry of gold and semiprecious stones.

015. Persian woman, workingman, and religious man. The woman wears a tunic with short sleeves pulled up and tied, forming gathers and a puffed sleeve. At her waist she wears a wide girdle, and over her head a shawl wrapped into a turban to help balance the basket of fruit she carries. She wears a nose ring and other jewelry. The workingman in the center wears a short tunic with a fringed shawl wrapped around his hips and held in place by a wide band of fabric. He wears short leather boots and a felt cap. The religious man on the right, dressed in typical Jewish style, wears a prayer shawl and cloak, both with tassels, over his tunic. On his forehead is a prayer box and strap. He wears Oriental-styled slippers.

016. Persian official, king, and attendant. Left, a Persian high official wears a robe of honor, a style borrowed from the Medes. It is a large rectangle of fabric, folded to form a front and back and belted to form large sleeves, which in this case have the edges tied together at the waistband. The skirt is pulled up and tucked into the waistband. He is also wearing a tall pleated fabric cap, buttoned shoes, and a jeweled neckband. Right, a Persian king wears a more elaborately structured robe of state with fitted shoulders and pleated sleeves (worn over a full-cut shirt). The king's robe is tucked up at the left side only. His attendant, also in a robe of honor, but wearing a felt cap, holds a parasol over the king's head.

017. Egypt, Old Kingdom; a king. Wearing the "Red Crown" of lower Egypt, the king wears a jeweled collar on his upper torso. Wrapped around his lower torso is a schenti. A jeweled loin pendant hangs from the front of his belt, with a fur tail hanging from the back.

018. Egypt, Old Kingdom; a king and a woman. The king wears a loincloth fashioned from pleated gold fabric. A symbolic lion's tail is attached to the back. From his waist hangs a stiffened triangle of embroidered fabric covered with a jeweled loin pendant. The king carries the royal crook and flail, signs of his authority. A jeweled club is tucked into his waistband. The woman wears a sheath with two shoulder straps. A jeweled pendant hangs from her neck. On her head is a ribbon circlet with gold feathers arranged to form a coronet.

019. Egypt, Old Kingdom; a painter, or scribe, and his wife. His simple knee-length schenti is made of coarse linen. He wears no protective head cover, indicating that he works indoors. The woman wears a checked kalasiris with wide shoulder straps. Instead of a collar, she wears bands of necklaces.

020. Egypt, Old Kingdom; a scribe and a woman. The man, probably a scribe, wears a knee-length kilt, the front of which is covered by a starched apron of the same fabric. A baton is tucked into his waist. The woman wears a striped sheath with broad shoulder straps, and a jeweled collar.

021. Egypt, Old Kingdom; a king and his wife. The king wears a schenti made of pleated fabric, fastened at the waist by a belt. During the Old Kingdom, men wore bare torsos. This king wears the "White Crown" of upper Egypt and the royal ceremonial false beard. His wife wears a striped sheath with narrow shoulder straps. She nurses her baby, whom she supports with a square of fabric wrapped into a sling.

022. Egypt, Old Kingdom; an Egyptian couple of rank. The man, wearing a ceremonial kilt, carries a spear, and has a cudgel, or club, tucked into his belt. A short wig covers his head. The woman, grinding grain on a hand mill, wears a tunic draped over one shoulder.

023. Egypt, Middle Kingdom; a man and a woman. The man wears a loincloth covered with a starched and stiffened triangle. At his neck is a jeweled collar and a pendant. His torso is bare. He carries a fish in a net bag. The woman, wearing a scale-patterned sheath with broad shoulder straps, carries a straw fan. Her wig has been corn-rolled and braided.

024. Egypt, Middle Kingdom; a king and a woman. The king's clothing, worn as priestly garb, reflects a transition into the New

Kingdom. Of sheer pleated linen, it is tied in the front to form a stiffened and embroidered loin pendant. On his head he wears the khat, a cloth wig cover that is pulled to the back and tied like a ponytail. On the front of the khat is a golden uraeus, a cobra emblem denoting power. Across the king's chest is a folded cloth which acts as a suspender. The woman wears a multicolored linen kalasiris, in the style of the Old Kingdom. She wears a mantle made of heavier linen, as well as a collar, diadem, bracelets, and a wig.

025. Egypt, New Kingdom; a queen. She wears a sheer mantle over a sheath. On her head rests the sacred vulture headdress of a queen. She carries a royal scourge and is bedecked in jewels, including a jeweled collar.

026. Egypt, New Kingdom; a king. He wears a blue wig adorned with a diadem and three golden uraei, as well as a false royal beard. His gold collar is set with blue and white stones. Under the collar is a mantle draped and tied at the chest. A jeweled red, blue, and gold loin panel hangs from his belt. He carries the royal scourge and crook.

027. Egypt, New Kingdom; a king. The king wears a cloth nemes, or wig cover, which is gathered in back like a plait. He wears a diaphanous linen robe over a schenti. A jeweled pendant hangs from his belt.

028. Egypt, New Kingdom; a princess and a slave. A jeweled circlet adorns the princess's braided wig. She wears a diaphanous mantle over a sheer, pleated sheath. The slave wears a fringed mantle around her shoulders, tied at the bosom, and an embroidered chastity belt.

029. Egypt, New Kingdom; a king. The king is wearing the nemes head cloth with an uraeus, a jeweled collar, and a sheer shawl. The schenti, which covers a sheer kilt, has a jeweled frontal pendant. He also wears a lector's sash and a decorative royal tail.

030. Egypt, New Kingdom; a queen. She wears the gold and jeweled vulture headdress, a broad jeweled collar, and a richly embroidered kalasiris.

031. Egypt, New Kingdom; a pharaoh and a slave. The pharaoh wears the royal "Blue Crown" trimmed in gold and studded with blue. Hanging from it is a scarlet neck cloth called a cheperesh. His vest is embroidered with the sacred vulture's wings in black, green, and gold. His collar is gold. He wears a long, sheer skirt draped to the front, and a multicolored belt with loin pendant. The slave, carrying lotus blossoms, wears a pale green, sheer cloth draped and tied at her waist.

032. Egypt, New Kingdom; a noble couple. Dressed for a funeral, the man wears a linen cloth that is draped over one shoulder and knotted at the chest. A second cloth is wrapped around his hips and arranged in the front to form a full loin pouch. The woman wears a sheer mantle over a pleated robe.

033. Egypt, New Kingdom; a queen. This queen is dressed in ceremonial robes. She wears a narrow blue-and-white striped tunic over a wide, sheer under-gown with red shoulder straps. Her gold collar and bracelets are set with green stones. Her headdress is decorated with a red sun disk, golden plumes, and goat horns. She wears a red bandeau of ribbon with the gold uraeus. She carries an ankh and a lotus scepter.

034. Egypt, New Kingdom; Osiris. According to legend, Osiris, originally the god of agriculture, was killed by the god of darkness and transformed into the god of the underworld. Shown here, he wears a gold crown with white plumes, and a white royal beard. He carries the royal scourge and hook. Following tradition, his skin is painted green. His robe is mauve with rose disks and purple fretting; the armbands and fringe are white.

035. Egypt, New Kingdom; a noblewoman and nobleman. This noblewoman wears a fringed sari-like garment made of pleated, sheer linen. Wrapped tightly around her, it covers one arm and is secured in front with a pin. Her wig has golden tassels at the end of each lock, and she wears a jeweled circlet. The man, probably an official of the court, wears a sheer, pleated shawl over his shoulders and arms. His long skirt, made of the same fabric, is arranged to form a full loin pouch in the front.

036. Egypt, New Kingdom; a slave and a musician. On the left, the slave dances and strums a guitarlike instrument. She wears a typical beaded collar and belt. Adorning her head is a decorated circlet, and her hair appears to be in loose corn-rolls. Her large disk earrings are a relatively new style. The harp player wears a long, sheer sheath. The draped mantle is caught and gathered beneath the bosom by a jeweled pin. On her hair, which is also corn-rolled, she wears a heavy circlet with a ribbon down the back and a perfumed cone.

037. Egypt, New Kingdom; a woman. This illustration shows how to drape and tie a square, sheer robe over a kalasiris.

038. Egypt, New Kingdom; a soldier and a woman. The soldier wears a cloth headpiece styled like the khat, but without a wig. He wears a shirt and loincloth. From his belt hangs a heart-shaped leather loin piece. He carries a shield, club, and spear. The woman wears a large square of coarse linen draped over one shoulder, tied at the waist.

039–040. Hair and headdress styles of ancient Egypt. a. Basic New Kingdom man's wig. **b.** A New Kingdom basic wig for women. The hair is corn-rolled and braided. **c.** Woman's wig, hair combed back. **d.** Court entertainer wearing a corn-rolled wig and perfumed cone atop her head. Jeweled circlet, collar, and large disk earrings. **e.** Woman's wig worn with a jeweled headband. **f.** Styled for a king with bands and uraeus. **g.** Cloth wig cover called a khat or nemes. **h.** Queen Nefertiti, with a shaved head, wears a flat-topped crown. **i.** Variation of the blue crown. **j.** "White Crown" of upper Egypt, dating from pre-dynastic times. **k.** Variation on the "White Crown" with side plumes, from the New Kingdom. **l.** Queen Hatshepsut wearing the royal vulture crown, topped with two plumes and a sun disk. **m.** Combined "White Crown" and "Red Crown." **n.** New Kingdom prince wearing the "Horus lock" of youth. His ceremonial crown depicts goat horns, papyrus bundles, and plumes. Both crown and headband have the uraeus. **o.** The pre-dynastic "Red Crown" of lower Egypt. **p.** Ceremonial chepheresh, or "Blue Crown," with gold studs and trim.

041. Cretan nobility, ca. 2000–1200 B.C. The Cretan ideal was a slim-waisted figure for both men and women. Men usually wore only a decorated loincloth, and often women did too, but sometimes women wore corseted jackets to enhance their slim waists. The bosom was left bare. The corselets and tiered skirts show considerable skill in dressmaking. Bright, primary colors and earth tones were favored.

042. Mycenaean common folk, ca. 1500–100 B.C. As in most civilizations, the common people wore a variation on the simple tunic. Archaeological fragments seem to indicate that the folk of Asia Minor decorated their tunics, which often were dyed in earth tones, with contrasting bands of fabric or embroidery.

043. Phrygian young woman and Amazon, ca. 1200–900 B.C. Both women's sewn and girdled gowns, the Amazon's tights, and the other's cloak and cap are delicately embroidered.

044. The Greek chiton, ca. 500 B.C. The man's chiton, sometimes called a camisia, had one girdle or belt. The woman's usually had two. The basic Greek chiton was folded down one side and open on the other. The back corners were pinned to the front to form shoulder straps. Chitons also could be floor length for both men and women.

045. The Doric peplos. Originally worn in the province of Doris, this form of the chiton was one of the basic Greek women's garments. A huge rectangle of fabric was first folded across the top, then folded down one side, and pinned at the shoulders. Just under the top flap it was girdled and bloused, and the draperies were carefully arranged.

046. The Ionic chiton. Another basic woman's garment, designed in the province of Ionia, this chiton was adopted throughout ancient Greece. It was an immense rectangle of fabric that was simply folded along one side and then pinned at intervals along the arms and at the shoulders. Girdled, it formed voluminous sleeves when carefully draped.

047. The Greek chlamys, ca. 500 B.C. Basically a large rectangle of fabric, this standard men's cloak was draped over the left shoulder and pinned on the right. It could be worn over a chiton or alone.

048. Fashionable Greek women, ca. 600–480. B.C. The woman on the left wears a variation on the Doric peplos; the other wears an arrangement of the Ionic chiton. Note the elaborate patterning, as well as their intricate hairstyles. The woman on the left has her hair bound in a bandeau, and her companion wears a coronet called a stephanie as well as a snoodlike affair to hold up her coiffure.

049. Greek warriors, ca. 440 B.C. The warrior on the left wears a soft linen chiton under his metal breastplate and short chain-mail skirt. His metal helmet with neck shield sports a plume of red horsehair, and he wears metal shin armor. The foot soldier of lower rank wears a short tunic with an overskirt in brightly colored linen. His metal helmet has a less impressive plume than his superior's.

050. Greek rustic couple, ca. 480 B.C. The girl wears an Ionic chiton, girdled and shortened, over a long, short-sleeved chiton, both of lightweight linen, which has been twisted while damp to form broomstick pleats. Her knit cap is held in place by a stephanie. The boy wears a short, broomstick-pleated chiton under a short chlamys with a sun hat hanging in back.

051. Banquet guest and dancing girl, ca. 500 B.C. Most Greek banquets were strictly male affairs, with the attendees reclining on couches to dine, wearing only the himation and garlands of flowers in their hair. Guests usually were entertained by musicians and female dancers. The young woman wears a sheer, patterned himation draped over one shoulder and falling in a train at the back.

052. Greek serving girl and matron, ca. 250 B.C. The serving girl is wearing a long chiton with a single girdle. On her head she wears a cloth cap. Her mistress's garb is a patterned Ionic chiton with a himation over the shoulder, girdled at the waist. Note the elaborate embroidered band on the edge of the himation and the weight on its corner. The weight enhanced the line of the drape.

053. Etruscan couple, ca. 1000 B.C. The Etruscan women wore sewn dresses, which either had a fitted peplos or a sewn jacket. The men seem to have worn a fitted long tunic with a cloak called a tabenna. Both men's and women's garments were decorated with broad stripes of color.

054. Etruscan couple, ca. 750 B.C. The woman's dress is belted and has a capelet, which is pinned at the shoulder. The man is wearing a tabenna, semicircular in cut, draped over his shoulders. The Etruscan men allowed their long hair to hang over their shoulders, sometimes braiding it in the back.

055. Roman patricians, ca. 750 B.C. These men are wearing the banded toga, seen here in one of its simplest drapes. Note the curve of its banded edge. The weights on the two bottom corners of each toga enable the graceful wave effect to remain in place.

056. Religious pilgrims, ca. 150 B.C. The man wears a long bordered toga over a short-sleeved long tunica. For religious ceremonies the toga was worn covering the head. Over a long tunica, the woman is wearing the palla, which differed from the semicircular toga by being rectangular in shape. She wears a veil.

057. Roman senator and woman, ca. 100–25 B.C. The statesman wears the classic toga over a long tunic. His companion wears an Ionic chiton of sheer fabric with a palla draped about her hips and over her arm. Her compact hairdo is crowned by a simple stephanie. Both wear leather sandals; his are partly enclosed.

058. Man and woman in everyday garb, ca. A.D. 25. The man wears a short tunica with long, fitted sleeves, and a short cloak. He wears high leather boots. The woman wears a tunica and a palla.

059. Roman centurion and high officer, ca. A.D. 150–200. The centurion wears metal scale armor over his pleated tunic, and metal greaves or shin armor. Over the scale armor he wears silver decorations of merit, suspended from ribbons. A mantle is draped over his left shoulder and arm. He carries a vinewood stick (the mark of a centurion) and his helmet. The officer wears leather armor and a leather skirt over a cloth tunic and knitted breeches. His mantle is of red-purple wool, and his helmet bears a "caterpillar" style crest. His shield is in the round "Greek style."

060. Germanic mercenary foot soldier and Roman horseman, ca. A.D. 100–250. The foot soldier wears a leather-fringed loincloth and decorated belts around his waist. Over his shoulders he wears a paenula with a hood. He is carrying a shield and a javelin, and wears a sword and a dagger. The horseman wears a simple tunica with a fitted shoulder cape, over knitted breeches. He has a metal helmet, a horseman's spear, a long sword, and a tooled and painted leather shield.

061. A Roman senator and his family, ca. A.D. 300–487. The woman wears a tunica with a band of a contrasting color down the front, under a palla draped over her shoulders. Her hair is elaborately curled and braided. The child is dressed in a toga like his father's, but not banded. By this time the toga had become narrower and much longer, allowing for more complex draping.

062. Gladiators and attendant, ca. A.D. 250–300. The attendant wears an unbelted tunica with a band of a contrasting color down the center. He is blowing a horn to announce the next contest. The net fighter in the center (a retiarius) wears only a belt and loincloth, leather greaves, a metal shoulder plate, and a chain-mail sleeve and glove. He carries a metal net and trident spear. The Thracian gladiator on the right carries a gladius (sword) and a shield. He wears a belted loincloth. His visored helmet, shoulder and arm protectors, and greaves all are of metal.

063. Grecian hairstyles and headgear, ca. 750–300 B.C. The sequence shows changes progressing from the ancient Archaic period to the Hellenic.

064. Roman hairstyles and headgear, ca. 300–100 B.C. A variety of hairpins and clasps are shown.

065. Constantine and the angel (fourth century). According to legend, Constantine I dreamed that an angel told him to go to battle under the Christian cross. The emperor followed the angel's advice and was victorious, his success leading to his founding the Byzantine Empire. Constantine's mantle and tunica were depicted in primary colors in Byzantine art, the angel's in pastel tones. The mantle is fastened in typical style over the right shoulder with a jeweled clasp. Constantine wears decorated slip-on shoes.

066. Fourth-century Byzantine woman and civil official. The woman is wearing a brightly colored long stola decorated with gold embroidery over a long-sleeved tunica. Her palla falls from a diadem of sheer linen or silk. The man, a civil official, wears a short, light-colored tunica with multicolored embroidery. His mantle of dark material has a decorative tablion. He wears light-colored stockings and brightly colored soft leather boots.

067. Fourth-century Christian commoners. The father and son depicted here wear short linen camisias. The boy's camisia was probably his "dress-up" wear; the vertical stripe appears on matching stockings. The father's light-colored camisia is worn for work, doubling as an undergarment when he dresses up in an over-tunica. His boots (calcei) are made of soft leather. When working in the fields, he probably dispensed with stockings.

068. Fourth-century Byzantine couple. In the early years of the Byzantine Empire, men did not always wear stockings. The man's tunica has embroidered trim. He wears leather thong sandals. The woman wears a brightly colored dalmatic with a multicolored, geometric-patterned, embroidered trim and a matching head scarf. Women's shoes typically were red throughout most of the Byzantine period.

069. Fourth-century royal couple. He wears a brocaded silk tunica under a dark cloak, fastened with a fibula. He has on dark stockings and shoes. She wears a pale silk camisia under a long tunica of brightly colored silk and a dark mantle.

070. Emperor Arcadius and a warrior. Left, Emperor Arcadius (ruled 395–408) is shown here dressed in a white camisia, worn under a woolen, silk-embroidered tunica and a polished metal lorica. He wears soft leather boots over bare legs. Right, the warrior wears a linen camisia, leather lorica, skirt, and armbands. He has

on wool stockings and leather shoes.

071. Fourth-century Byzantine couple. The man wears a short, light-colored tunica over dark trousers. His cloak, cut to free the arm, is held with two fasteners. The woman wears a loose dalmatic-style tunica over a light-colored camisia. Her tunica and palla are embroidered in bright colors.

072. Fifth-century Byzantine couple. The woman wears a long-sleeved linen camisia under an embroidery-trimmed dalmatic. Her slip-on shoes have a geometric design as well. The man wears a linen camisia, cloth hose with ties, and soft leather boots dyed a bright color.

073. Emperor Justinian and Empress Theodora. Emperor Justinian (ruled 527–565) and Empress Theodora represented the apex of Byzantine splendor and style. Both wear heavily jeweled crowns embellished with ropes of pearls. Their mantles and tunicas are heavily embroidered with gold thread. Both cloaks are fastened with ornate, jeweled fibulae. Gold embroidery, worked with beads and jewels, appealed to the wealthy, who favored deep, rich hues for their mantles—plum, dark green, black, and, for members of royalty, deep purple.

074. Empress Theodora. Shown here are two costumes attributed to Theodora. In her day, she was considered to be the most beautiful, as well as the most powerful, woman in the world. Left, Theodora wears a patterned stola over a jeweled, embroidered camisia, topped by a jeweled collar and belt. Her palla is made of sheer silk edged with teardrop pearls. Right, the empress wears a semicircular palla, edged with pearls and decorated with an embroidered religious tablion. Her coif and collar feature large pearls and precious stones.

075. Galla Placida and Emperor Valentinian III. Galla Placida was the half-sister of Emperor Arcadius and the mother of Emperor Valentinian III (he ruled the western Roman Empire from 425 to 455, after the division of the empire into east and west). Galla Placida wears a camisia with jeweled sleeves under a long, brightly colored silk tunica and a palla of royal purple. Her son, Valentinian III, is wearing a brocaded tunica, as well as a brocaded mantle fastened with a fibula. His stockings and slippers are brightly colored.

076. Sixth-century men of rank. Two men of rank, both wearing brightly colored silk tunicas. The man on the left wears a tunica with pleats in the back, over a long camisia. The man on the right wears a ceremonial toga over his long camisia.

077. Sixth-century noble couple. The man is dressed in a short mantle worn over a tunica with a decorative apron. His tight-fitting trousers are made of brocade and are, like his tunica and mantle, heavily trimmed with embroidery. His Phrygian cap is made of brightly colored felt. The woman wears an embroidered dalmatic over a long camisia. Her flowing silk palla is the same color as her camisia.

078. Seventh-century cavalryman and foot soldier. A cavalryman and a foot soldier show the subtle differences in military costume. The cavalryman (left) wears long, fitted sleeves with leather armbands. His cloak is shorter and he wears hose, whereas the foot soldier is bare legged; the cavalryman's shield is smaller than the oblong one carried by the foot soldier. Their helmets are generally the same, but the cavalryman has a feather crest.

079. Seventh-century warrior and townswoman. The warrior wears a dark wool cloak and a dark felt cap with light edging. He wears a leather tunica and skirt, bare legs, light-colored socks, and dark shoes. The townswoman wears a light-colored camisia under a pale cloak with embroidered neckline, and soft red leather shoes.

080. Seventh-century courtier and priest. Left, the courtier wears a brightly colored short tunica with embroidered sleeves over his light-colored camisia and cloth leggings; an embroidered purse hangs from his belt. His mantle has a richly embroidered border and tablion and is fastened with a fibula. He wears tall leather boots with open toes. Right, the priest wears a long camisia under his tunica; the circular mantle is topped by a lorum embroidered with crosses.

081. Emperor Romanus II and Empress Eudokia. These images of Emperor Romanus II (ruled 959–963) and his first wife, Empress Eudokia, are derived from a late-eleventh-century ivory carving, once thought to depict Romanus IV and his wife, Empress Eudoxia. Here, the emperor and empress wear splendidly ornate costumes embroidered with pearls. Their crowns are embellished with ornamental pendants.

082. Emperor Nicephorus III and his empress. After the reign of Otto III the Greeks regained the empire, and their taste for lavish decoration was reestablished. Emperor Nicephorus III (ruled 1078–1081) and his empress are shown wearing gold brocade coronation robes with embroidered trim. A multicolored jeweled lorum is wrapped across the emperor's chest and hips. The empress has a jeweled collar and jeweled woman's version of the lorum wrapped around her hips.

083. Eleventh-century royal robes. The empress's dark gown is adorned in the front with a light-colored decorative panel. Multicolored embroidery enhances the ensemble. The emperor is wearing his military apparel, consisting of a dark cloak worn over a white, long-sleeved camisia, a metal lorica, a short tunica with embroidered trim, and cloth stockings. His boots are leather, studded with jewels.

084. Eleventh-century court dancer. This performer is dressed in a brightly colored brocaded silk gown with exaggerated bell sleeves. Her hat of brightly colored straw is accented with multicolored brocaded bands. She wears red slippers.

085. Eleventh-century upper-class woman. The women of the upper classes were rarely seen in public; nevertheless, the robes that they wore at home were constructed of fine fabrics and were richly jeweled and embroidered. On the right, the woman is depicted almost entirely covered by her palla, a garment required when she left the home. The palla was generally of a very dark color, whereas the gown would have displayed brighter, more jewel-like tones.

086. Twelfth-century merchant and monk. Left, the merchant wears a short juppe (shirt) with embroidered sleeve cuffs and a light-colored belt. Under the juppe he wears a short tunica, Persian-style trousers with a multicolored embroidered panel, and colorful medium-height stockings and leather shoes. Right, the monk's garments consist of a dark mantle, a light-colored short tunica with embroidered medallions, dark cloth stockings, and leather shoes.

087. Women's hairstyles of the Byzantine Empire. a–d. 6th c. **e.** 5th c. **f.** 4th c. **g.** Earring. **h.** 11th c. **i.** 6th c. **j.** 7th c. **k.** Earring. **l.** Fibula. **m.** 10th c. **n.** Earring. **o.** 5th c. **p.** 7th c. **q.** 12th c. **r.** 13th c. **s.** 6th c.

088. Men's hairstyles of the Byzantine Empire. a–b. 6th c. **c–d.** 9th c. **e.** 11th c. **f.** 10th c. **g.** 11th c. **h–i.** 12th c. **j.** Lorum. **k.** 10th c. **l.** 12th c. **m.** Tablion. **n.** 14th c.

089. Celtic-Norse couple, ca. 1000 B.C. They are both wearing skins, fur side out. He has bronze buckles and jewelry and wears an elaborately decorated dagger. He is carrying a club. The woman is carrying a spear and a helmet, probably indicating that she is a skilled hunter and fighter .

090. Frankish family, ca. 800 B.C. The woman wears a long, short-sleeved tunic over a long gown, and a gold headband, bracelets, belt, and necklace. The bosom of her tunic is decorated with embroidery in a spiral design. The man wears a chain-link and leather vest over a short-sleeved tunic. On his legs he wears soft leather leggings which are gartered with leather strips below the knee. He carries a spear and wears a metal-link belt with an elaborately decorated broad sword. From his back hangs a wood-and-metal shield. The little boy wears a soft leather short tunic, fur in, and leather leggings like his father's.

091. Teutonic couple, ca. 800 B.C. He wears a long belted tunic with elbow-length sleeves. She wears a short tunic over a long skirt. Her soft leather belt has long fringe hanging from its bottom edge. Both wear "sunflower"-shaped decorative bronze belt buckles. Both also wear soft leather laced-up shoes. People had to make their own shoes rather frequently because they did not have a separate sole of hardened leather.

092. Teutons, ca. 800 B.C. Her long-sleeved tunic is enhanced by a metal collar with raised geometric designs as well as a belt with a large metal sunflower disk. He wears a short leather-belted tunic under a knee-length wool cape pinned with a gold fibula. Under his leather-strip sandals he wears short knit stockings. Her hair is confined with a coarse fishnet-type snood and he wears a wool or felt cap.

093. Migrating nomadic tribe, ca. 400 B.C. One of the constant traits of the North European nomadic tribes was the urge to move on to greener pastures. The causes could be many—defeat by an enemy, the search for richer lands, or possibly an exploding population. The woman wears a hooded cloak over a long plaid woolen tunic and carries her child, who wears a tunic and has a shawl. The man wears a heavy wool cloak over a woolen tunic and the boy has a hooded cloak over a tunic. Both man and boy wear leggings of sheepskin bound with leather thongs.

094. A European or Gallic farmer, ca. 300 B.C. He wears a wool tunic with bold checks over long breeches that are gathered at the ankles. He is greeting a neighbor, possibly his landlord, who is riding in a wicker-and-wood cart with his wife and son. The woman wears a long-sleeved belted tunic and a shawl, the boy wears a belted tunic, and the father is dressed the same as the farmer except that he wears a gold torque at his neck—a sign of status.

095. Migrating chieftain and warrior, ca. 400 B.C. The chieftain wears a fur tunic and leggings over a wool under-tunic and leather trousers. The warrior wears coarse-textured woolen breeches, a wool tunic, and a long cloak. He carries a wooden shield. Their trousers could have been a carry-over from their ancient near-eastern origins, or simply developed independently from the fact that they were horsemen and needed leg covering for protection.

096. Gallic couple in a metalsmith's workshop, ca. 300 B.C. The lady wears a short-sleeved plaid wool belted tunic and is admiring a bronze mirror. The man wears a short-sleeved tunic over plaid wool bracchae (breeches), and the smith wears an apron of soft leather. In barbarian society the smith had almost supernatural status and was considered as much a sorcerer as a craftsman.

097. British-Celtic warriors, ca. 150 B.C. Two of the warriors are shown in the nude except for foot covering, helmets, weapons, and shields. One, probably a farmer who has joined in the battle, wears plaid bracchae and shoes. He brandishes a spear with a skull on it. The Celts often cut off the heads of their enemies and displayed the skulls as prized trophies. The man with the helmet is probably the chieftain, and his helmet has horns that represent the ox. He also wears a golden torque around his neck.

098. Gallic warriors, ca. 100 B.C. The warrior on the left wears wool bracchae, and about his shoulders a sagum, which was a cape made of a folded rectangle of wool, pinned by a thorn. When opened out it was used as a blanket. On his head he wears a horned helmet. He carries a single-edged sword which probably means that he was a mercenary for the Romans. The warrior on the right wears a long-sleeved striped wool tunic with a broad attached collar-cape and bracchae. On his head he wears a cap of long fur and around his neck is an embossed bronze gorget and gold necklace. He is holding a horn whose bell is shaped like an animal head. His shield is of wood and boiled leather and he wears a sword.

099. Serfs, ca. 49 B.C. By the time of Rome's conquest and occupation of the British Isles, ca. 49 B.C., there was little difference in the dress of the two peoples. The common folk generally wore plaid woolen tunics and/or breeches and skirts.

100. Celtic Druids. According to Roman reports the Druids dressed in long white robes. There are some reports that there were female Druids who dressed in black. The Druids held their religious ceremonies in wooded glades and made offerings to the gods by casting donated jewelry or other prized possessions into sacred springs or streams.

101. Gallic warriors, ca. A.D. 100. Often the Celts became mercenaries for the Roman army. The man on the left is a foot soldier using a slingshot, while the man on the right wears a Romanized version of battle attire, although he still wears the Celtic or barbarian hair and beard style and a torque about his neck.

102. British warriors, ca. A.D. 500. By A.D. 407, Rome had withdrawn her troops from Britain and Ireland, leaving them vulnerable to invasions by groups such as the Saxons, the Picts, and the Vikings. Dressing much like their invaders, these warriors both wear leather and metal body armor over bracchae and metal helmets. The warrior on the left has fur-lined leggings and carries a battle-ax.

103. British women, ca. A.D. 600. These women are shown carding, spinning, and weaving. The seated women's costumes are of the medieval style with fitted bodice. The standing woman wears a shirt with a skirt, both in colorful plaids. The child is wrapped in a plaid scarf.

104. British chieftain and soldier, A.D. 500.

105. Frankish warrior and woman. The Franks were a Germanic people (related to the Vikings) who invaded western Europe about 500 A.D. They were fierce fighters. Here we see a Frankish warrior dressed in a short, sleeveless, belted fur tunic over a short skirt, wearing a mantle fastened at the left shoulder. The Franks often dyed their hair bright red in order to seem more ferocious and terrifying. The woman wears a short tunic with bell shaped sleeves over a long under-tunic or gunna (gown).

106. Charlemagne and a lady. Charlemagne preferred plainer dress than the Byzantine fashions of Papal Rome. Here he wears a soft, long-sleeved tunic or shirt, under a short-sleeved tunic embellished with embroidered trim, and a mantle over his shoulders. He wears linen braes under gartered stockings and short leather boots. His lady is wearing a straight-cut gown with a colored insert trim and an embroidered mantle over her head and shoulders that is caught around the waist.

107. Angles and Saxons, 10th century. The Angles and the Saxons were tribes who left the continent and ruled England from the fifth century to the Norman Conquest in 1066. They wore a variety of tunics and mantles, both long and short, narrow and wide. The women wore gowns to the floor and long mantles that covered the head.

108. Normans, 10th century. The Normans were Vikings from Scandinavia who migrated south to France, eventually adopting Christianity and the French language. They eventually spread to Italy, Sicily, England, Wales, and Scotland. The short tunic of the Normans and the Anglo-Saxons were nearly identical, but in the eleventh century the robes and gowns of the Normans took on a Byzantine influence with flared cuffs and hems caught up into waistbands.

109. Ninth-century noblewomen. Left, the Frankish noblewoman wears a mantle over a mail girdle with mail sleeves over a bliaud. Right, the Norman noblewoman is wearing a mantle, bliaud, and chainse.

110. Tenth-century Frankish nobility. The Frankish noblewoman wears an embroidered mantle over a bliaud and chainse. The nobleman is wearing a mantle over an embroidered tunic, cross-gartered stockings, and soft leather shoes.

111. Eleventh-century soldier and knight. Left, the foot soldier wears a short tunic, cross-gartered tights, and leather shoes. A chain-mail hood covers his iron skullcap. Over his chest he wears a leather baldric, a diagonal sash for carrying a shield and knife; he holds a battle-ax. Right, the crusader knight is wearing a metal battle helmet, or spangenhelm, over a chain-mail hood. He wears a soft under-tunic or pourpoint covered by his tunic of hardened leather tiles. His arms and legs are protected by fitted chain-mail sleeves and leggings; his shoes are leather.

112. Eleventh-century peasants. Under her cloak, the woman wears a bliaud covered with an apron laced for fit. She wears cross-gartered, soft leather stockings. On her head is a headrail. The man wears a short tunic over loose drawers which are cross-gartered. His cloak is tied at the shoulder. On his head he wears a peaked cloth or Phrygian helmet-shaped cap. His shoes are leather.

113. Twelfth-century merchant and noblewoman. The commoner merchant wears a belted surcoat over a bliaud. His mantle fastens at the shoulder; a pouch hangs from his belt or girdle. On his head

is a conical felt hat. The woman wears a short-sleeved bliaud over a full-sleeved chemise, and a long mantle over all. The mantle and bliaud are edged with jeweled embroidery. Her headgear includes a conical hennin, or high headdress, over her headrail, or veil.

114. Twelfth-century Frankish royalty. The Frankish prince wears a long, elaborately embroidered bliaud with extremely long sleeves, perhaps to keep his hands warm. His chainse is floor length. Tied at the shoulder, his mantle has an embroidered band at the bottom. The princess wears an outfit with finely embroidered trim. Circling her long bliaud is a double girdle of jeweled leather with silk ties.

115. Twelfth-century French commoners. The hunter wears a short tunic with batwing or dolman sleeves. Bloused fabric at his waist covers a belt. He wears knitted stockings, low cut leather shoes, and a felt hat. A wicker quiver hangs from his waist and he holds a long bow. Carrying a shoulder scarf or stole, the townswoman wears a belted bliaud with dolman sleeves. Her headrail is wrapped like a turban.

116. Thirteenth-century knight and lady. The crusader knight wears a chain-mail hood under a steel helmet with a chain mail tunic, leggings, steel knee guards and shoes. Over the tunic he wears a surcoat with dagged edging. The English noblewoman is wearing a white linen wimple and gorget with a jeweled circlet. Her diaper-pattern bliaud covers a white chemise. Covering all is a full mantle with contrasting lining.

117. Thirteenth-century nobility. The waist of the noblewoman's gown has moved to just under the bosom; the skirt has an extremely long train. She wears a steeple hennin with a loose veil. The gentleman's cote, or jacket, is cut short, showing his legs to advantage. Featuring padded and puffed shoulders and slashed hanging sleeves, his cote has a fur-trimmed collar. Around his neck he wears a circlet of fur.

118. Thirteenth-century German upper-class couple. The maid wears a front-laced, diapered surcoat over a heavily embroidered short-sleeved bliaud and simple chemise. On her head is a jeweled circlet. The lack of a headrail or wimple indicates that she is a maiden. The man wears a hood with a liripipe under his cape and tunic. He wears wool tights and soft leather, fur-trimmed boots.

119. Fourteenth-century French nobility. This lady wears a pale-colored cote-hardie, girdled at the hip. Her brightly colored surcoat has hanging sleeves and miniver trim. The lord wears a bag cap with a padded, rolled brim and a jeweled ornament. His jacket is brocaded silk with velvet sleeves; his tights and shoes are parti-colored.

120. Fourteenth-century Flemish nobility. The gentleman wears a shoulder cape hood with a liripipe over a cote-hardie with a matching hem. The cote-hardie is accessorized with ermine cuffs and a jeweled belt. He wears dark stockings and embroidered shoes. The gentlewoman wears a diaper-pattern cote-hardie covering a white tunic. Her silk hennin has a braided net.

121. Fourteenth-century English princess and lady-in-waiting. Left, the lady-in-waiting wears a belted bliaud over an embroidered chainse. The sleeves are the same fabric as the bliaud. Right, the princess wears a fitted cote trimmed in ermine over an embroidery-edged bliaud. Her mantle is brocaded, lined with ermine. On the sides of her head she wears cylinder cauls topped by a crown over a peaked cap.

122. Fourteenth-century English king and page. The king wears a brocaded tunic, a shirt with long sleeves, and knitted tights with feet. Petal-scallops edge his mantle and he wears his jeweled girdle at his hip. The page wears a girdle at his waist; his sleeves are angel style.

123. Fourteenth-century French nobleman. This gentleman wears a fur-lined houppelande of brocaded silk with castellated edges on the Dalmatian sleeves. The skirt is slit at the sides with dagged ribbons trailing down the back. His hat is chaperon style.

124. Fourteenth-century French noblewoman. The lady's silk brocade houppelande has a sheer over-cape. Her skirt and cuffs are edged with fur bands that match the plumed fur hat.

125. Fifteenth-century English noblewoman. The lady wears a fur-lined houppelande over a gown of gold brocaded silk. Around her neck she wears a jeweled necklace. Her rolled, heart-shaped, silk hennin is embellished with a jeweled net reticulated caul.

126. Fifteenth-century French nobility. This nobleman wears a houppelande with petal scalloping. His hat is a padded roundlet with chaperon. The lady wears a gown and hennin of metal-shot silk, trimmed with a boldly colored velvet hatband, collar, cuffs, hem, and jewel-studded belt. Her sheer veil is wired to hold its butterfly shape.

127. Fourteenth-century Italian upper-class couple. She wears a gown with a jeweled bodice and a fur-edged, front slit skirt over a brocade underskirt. The enormous dogaline sleeves are lined with soft fur. On her head is a stuffed satin turban. His houppelande has embroidered cuffs and a fur-trimmed bottom edge. Topping his linen cap is a felt hat with a peaked brim and feather.

128. Fourteenth-century Italian nobility. The lady wears a brocaded robe with long flowing sleeves and a train. Her wimple and padded silk hennin are bound with gimp and trimmed with fur. The man wears a short tunic with a gold, enameled, and jeweled girdle. His mantle is doubled and puffed around his shoulders.

129. Fifteenth-century German nobility. The noblewoman wears a silk robe with an embroidered pattern. The fitted bodice and the skirt hem are trimmed in ermine. On her head she wears a steeple hennin with a black lappet band covering the lower edge. Showing at her forehead is a frontlet ring that is part of the wire cap under her hennin. The gentleman wears a knee-length cote-hardie. The shirt fabric is pulled through the spaces between the buttons on the sleeves to create puffs. He wears a petal-dagged chaperon with a petal-edged liripipe hanging down the front.

130. Fifteenth-century German nobility. This lady wears a gown with full bag sleeves under a mantle with a cord closure. On her head is a padded turban with a jeweled pin. The veil tabs have castellated edges. The gentleman wears a brocaded houppelande with padded shoulders and long, exaggerated sleeves. He wears dark shoes, tights, and a felt sugarloaf hat.

131. Fifteenth-century French peasants. The woman wears a robe with a fitted waist, the result of lacing in the back. Her skirt hem is tucked into the band around her hips to protect it from getting dirty, exposing her chainse. On her head she wears a cloth cap with a rolled headband. Over his shirt and braes, the man wears a laced cote that is open at the sides. His leather stockings are held up with leather rope. He wears a wide-brimmed straw hat.

132. Twelfth-century headdresses. a. Long plaits bound with ribbons with metal cylinders covering the ends. **b.** Phrygian or close-fitting cloth cap. **c.** A peaked hat made of felt with castellated brim. **d.** Linen gorget, or collar. **e.** Folded wimple worn over chin strap cap. **f.** Wimple. **g.** Hood and cape. **h.** White linen toque with pie-crust edging worn over chin-band. **i.** Jeweled velvet toque worn over gorget and chin-band. **j.** Chin-band and toque of pleated linen. **k.** Toque worn over a chin-strap cap with net caul covering hair. **l.** Chin-band and headband of ribbon. **m.** Turban with moiré leaves. **n.** White linen cap and chin-band under a gold crown. **o.** Men's version of the wimple with banded wool cap.

133. Thirteenth-century headgear and coifs. a. Embroidered linen toque with chin-band. **b.** Embroidered hennin with black velvet fold worn over a white cap and front loop. **c.** Two-horned English hennin. **d.** Pleated linen toque with chin-band. **e.** White linen headrail drawn through crownless toque. **f.** Jeweled circlet over crocheted wool net. **g.** Chin-band wimple and castellated linen toque. **h.** Straw hat worn over soldier's chain-mail hood. **i.** Broad-brimmed felt hat worn over a wimple and veil. **j.** Modified, stuffed and rolled hennin with padded circlet. **k.** Man's toque with tie-on chin-band. **l.** Rolled-under hairdo and beard of the period. **m.** Felt hat worn over cap with chin-band. **n.** Wimple with chin-band and circlet.

134. Fourteenth-century headdresses. a. Gorget or wimple with a sheer veil worn as a headrail with a pearl circlet. Hair is looped over the ears. **b.** Gorget and gathered headrail tucked onto a headband. **c.** Cylindrical cauls worn with a chin-band. **d.** Jeweled circlet with sheer headrail. **e.** Stuffed, rolled, and jeweled hennin worn with reticulated cauls and veil. **f.** Widow's mourning pleated barb, worn over the chin, with mourning veil. **g.** Simple headrail. **h.** Headrail pinned up in the style of a chaperon. **i.** Man's hood with liripipe and shoulder cape. **j.** Man's felt cap worn over a coif cap with chin-strap. **k.** Man's felt hat, page boy haircut. **l.** Man's sugarloaf hat worn over a hood. **m.** Man's conical felt hat. **n.** Man's hood with caul. **o.** Man's felt hat with peaked brim. Worn over a cap, it is topped with a feather.

135. Fifteenth-century women's headgear. a. Steeple hennin, particolored, with frontlet, worn over a headrail of veiling. A soft veil hangs from the point of the hennin. **b.** Headdress of reticulated gold braid and pearls with drum cauls. **c.** Jeweled linen turban with veil and heron plumes. **d.** Felt embroidered toque with wired veil. **e.** Escoffion, or two-horned hennin, made of brocaded silk, edged with pearls. Soft veil. **f.** Padded linen turban with jewels, pearls, and gold braid. A liripipe hangs from the turban to the floor in back. **g.** Jeweled cap with wired veil. **h.** Wimple with castellated edge over reticulated cauls. **i.** Jeweled crown over reticulated caul. **j.** Diaper-patterned steeple hennin with wired veil and gorget attached to band. Veil edged with brocaded band.

136. Fifteenth-century men's headgear. a. Felt hat with braided bandeau and peacock feathers. **b.** Cap-cut hairstyle. **c.** Roundlet with dagged chaperon and liripipe. **d.** Chaperon turban. **e.** Cloth hat with page boy haircut. **f.** Cloth hat with turned-up brim and jeweled pin. **g.** Felt sugarloaf hat with rolled brim, jeweled pin, feather, and cord hatband. **h.** Velvet bag hat with rolled brim. **i.** Wool peaked hat with set-on peaked brim. **j.** Felt hat with cap crown, rolled brim, and feather.

137. Italy, ca. 1400. The woman wears an "Italian gown" with fitted bodice and attached sleeves in rich red-and-gold brocade. Her turbanlike beret is of similar brocade. The man wears a short, dark-blue doublet under a short blue gown with attached gold-trimmed full sleeves. He has a gold satin muff and wears particolor red-and-white knit hose. Primary colors and other bright colors were popular at this time.

138. Italy, Venetian man and woman, ca. 1400. His parti-color hose are red, yellow, and black. His short, red-satin gown has a black fur collar and full, slashed sleeves. His gold-color doublet is laced over a white shirt and he wears yellow kid gloves. It was fashionable for young men to wear their hair long. The young woman wears a pale-blue silk, high-waisted short gown with a side slit to show her rose-color petticoat. Her tied-on sleeves are called "finestrella" because the chemise shows through. Unmarried girls could wear their necklines low.

139. Italy, Milanese couple, ca. 1410. The young woman wears a high-waisted gown of lavender taffeta with attached finestrella sleeves, both elaborately embroidered in silver and gold. Her petticoat is of wine-and-gold brocade. White chemise and cap; white feather fan. The youth wears a short tunic with rolled and padded gathering in the front. His apparel is pale blue with gold trim.

140. Italy, ca. 1410. This young Neapolitan man wears waist-high scarlet hose and a soft white shirt with a blue-gray gown that has blue-and-gold slashed sleeves. At his waist is a leather purse. His hat is of light-gray felt. The young woman wears a gown of pale-rose moiré trimmed in gold embroidery, as are her finestrella sleeves. Over one shoulder she wears a long shawl, folded and stitched to provide arm openings. She wears a white cloth cap; her long hair is bound with rose ribbons.

141. Germany and France, ca. 1420. The German gentleman on the left wears light-blue tights, a darker blue doublet with ermine trim, and a burgundy cloak with gold embroidery and ermine lining. The Frenchman on the right is wearing white hose with a fur-collared rose gown embroidered in gold and purple. He wears a gold-slashed doublet with blue embroidery and a white shirt with blue-and-gold embroidery at the neck. These garments illustrate that the Italian style was adapted for colder northern climates by the early 1400s.

142. Italy, ca. 1420. The noblewoman wears a robe of green silk-velvet with gray fur trim. The padded sleeves of her gown are of magenta silk-taffeta. Her hat is of magenta silk with gold net. The knight in armor has a tabard of red, blue, and gold wool in front and of gray fur in back. His hat is of red felt.

143. Italy, ca. 1430. This woman's plum-color velvet gown features hanging bag sleeves and is trimmed with white fur. Her underskirt is of saffron silk. The hat is of the same plum as the gown, with saffron slashes. The man is wearing a plum-colored short doublet with balloon sleeves. It is trimmed in white fur. Pale-blue stockings and a blue hat adorned with white feathers.

144. Italy, ca. 1440. The gentleman wears a short houppelande of wine-and-gold brocade with cape-like sleeves. Its bottom edging is scallops of wine, black, and gold. Gold chaperon with a liripipe. The woman's houppelande is of peacock blue-and-gold brocade with trim of gold, deep blue, and green. The undergown is of gold silk and the sleeves are edged in white fur. Her blond hair is held with strands of pearls.

145. Italy, ca. 1440. This high-waisted silk gown features leaf-shaped dagging at the sleeves. The gown is in shades of moss-green and gold. The man wears parti-color hose in red, yellow, and black, with the tunic repeating the same colors. His shirt and the fur trim are white.

146. Italy, ca. 1450. Italian peasant couple dressed for their wedding day. The bride wears a white chemise with a gold-and-dark-green busk (corset). The sleeves are dark green. Her skirt is dark blue and her petticoat is red wool with blue-and-yellow embroidery. She wears a natural-straw hat. The groom's costume includes a blue-gray doublet, brown breeches, a white shirt and stockings, tan leather slashed shoes, and a natural-straw hat.

147. Italian couple, ca. 1460. Her gown of coral-and-gold brocaded silk is worn over an underdress of slate-blue silk. Her embroidered cap is of matching colors. He is wearing a rose-and-blue hose under a wine-color gown with a gold lining. His sleeves are blue and gold and his cap is deep blue.

148. Lady and minstrel, ca. 1490. The lady wears a garland over her flowing hair, and her mantle features false sleeves that reveal the sleeves of her dress, which are fitted below the elbow. The minstrel wears a short gown with huge dagged sleeves, set-in and puffed at the shoulder. His stockings are parti-colored and are decorated with golden embroidered flames.

149. Prosperous English family, ca. 1494. The gentleman wears two gowns, the inner one lined with fur and the outer one of patterned silk with false sleeves. His shirt is seen at the neck and puffed through the doublet's sleeves (doublet is only visible at that point). The lady wears a very simply cut dress with full sleeves and a train whose edge is caught up in the chain girdle. On her head she wears a hood of simple cut. The child wears a patterned silk gown with a bib pinned on front and a cap under the hood.

150. Italy, Venetian lady and dandy, ca. 1500. She is dressed in a gown of sky-blue silk edged with silk fringe, over a pink-and-gold brocaded petticoat. At her neck is a white voile scarf, and she carries a white handkerchief. The colors of her embroidered and jeweled felt cap match the rest of her ensemble. The Venetian dandy is wearing blue-and-gold parti-color hose. His white shirt is pulled through and puffed at the sleeves, waist, back, and sides of the brocaded doublet, which has smaller slashes showing the wine-color lining. His cap is dark-blue velvet with gold trimmings.

151. English noble and lady, ca. 1500. He wears a full-length gown of gray-and-blue brocaded silk with light-brown fur trim, over a deep-red doublet, and parti-color hose. His codpiece is red and deep brown. His fur cap has multicolor feathers and gold braid. She wears a gown of rose silk with velvet brocade, trimmed with dark-brown fur. Her gabled coif is of jewels and gold and has a black velvet fall. Her girdle is gold silk, knotted and tasseled.

152. English country couple, ca. 1500. Country folks' work clothes were of rough fabrics, usually wool and coarse linens. The woman wears a long skirt with an overskirt. Her apron is tucked up under her belt, and she wears a plain scarf. Hanging from her belt are her knife and a leather purse. The man wears a leather jerkin over hose and tall soft leather boots that can be pulled up and attached to an underbelt in inclement weather.

153. England, ca. 1500. English lord and lady dancing after a hunting trip. His green-red-and-yellow plaid doublet has a long skirt and is worn over fitted green trunk hose and red stockings. His light-brown leather leggings are slashed; his shoes are of the same color. He wears a brown castellated cap over a white coif. The lady's riding outfit is of red wool, bound and belted in gold ribbon; her sleeves and coif are of quilted green silk. Her dark-green velvet hat has red and yellow feathers. Both have purses of natural leather.

154. Two English dandies, ca. 1500. These dandies are wearing white shirts with a gathered edging at the neck under their short paltocks (doublets). Left, the young man's gown is fur lined and has long false sleeves. He wears a linen cap under a broad-brimmed hat with plumes; pearls have been sewn onto the feathers' quills. Because of the size and weight of the hat, it must be tied under his chin. Right, the man wears a gown that is slit open like a cape and has capelike folds over the shoulders. He wears a simple velvet cap with an upturned brim.

155. English government officials, ca. 1504. Three officials wearing three different gown lengths. Left, a medium-length gown with a fur-trimmed cape collar. Center, a short gown with fur collar and cuffs, worn over a brocaded jerkin and taffeta doublet. Right, a long gown with lynx lining (when fur lined, the gown was often called a pelisse or pelican) worn over an undergown, or petticoat. His broad-brimmed fur cap is worn over a linen cap. They all wear variations on the broad-toed shoe.

156. Tudor gentleman and lady, ca. 1504. The man wears a full-sleeved gown over an undergown. The gown's neckline is elaborately embroidered; over his shoulders is a double necklace of golden cord. His long scarf is gathered at his waist and draped over his arm. The lady wears a linen cap with side lappets; her hood is folded up and over her head. Her full-sleeved gown is edged with embroidery, its square neck bordered with pearls. Her underrobe has full bag sleeves; beneath are the narrower pearl-edged sleeves of her chemise. Gold cord necklace and girdle.

157. England, ca. 1510. This English lady's dark-green velvet gown is lined and trimmed with white fur. The train of the gown is caught up and tied to the girdle by means of points (laces with metal tips, sometimes called aiglets, used to tie various parts of the costume together). Her undergown is pale green banded with black, and the fall and lappets to her coif are of black velvet. The gentleman wears a rust-color velvet gown with slashed sleeves. It is lined with darker-brown wool. His short, slashed green doublet is laced to his green-and-gold upper stocks, which are worn with shorter white stockings. A white shirt, white fur hat with multicolor feathers, and brown leather shoes complete his outfit.

158. Germany, ca. 1510. During the Renaissance, the Germans seemed to enjoy outdoing everyone else in the use of feathers, slashes, and puffs in their costume. The woman here wears a large-brimmed hat, edged in embroidery and covered with red, green, and gold feathers. Her pale-green silk gown has fur (animal-tail) trim around the skirt, and her attached gold sleeves (slashed) are banded in the green silk of the gown. She displays her bright-red petticoat. Her partner is swathed in a rose-and-yellow cloak worn over yellow-and-blue parti-color hose. His cap is of black velvet and is decorated with wired feathers in rose, yellow, and blue.

159. Germany, ca. 1510. This German soldier, in a slashed and puffed uniform, wears a blue doublet over a white shirt. Over the doublet is a tan leather jerkin with puffed sleeves showing the red lining of the garment. He also wears an apron of pale-blue fabric with gold-embroidered trim. His breeches are the same color as the doublet. His parti-color stockings are red and white on one leg, red and blue on the other. His castellated hat is brown and sports red and blue feathers. His brown shoes show red through the slashings. The woman's gown is of scarlet, with puffs of white chemise showing. The skirt of the gown is edged with gold braid, as is the hem of the blue petticoat. Her coif consists of loops of blue ribbon, trimmed with wired red and yellow ostrich plumes.

160. France, ca. 1510. The gentleman wears a brocaded pale-blue-and-gold cloak, lined with fur. His doublet is gold brocade, slashed to show the white shirt, which has red, blue, and gold embroidery at the neck. His stockings, trunk hose, and codpiece are red, with gold and blue bands. The woman's gown is gold-and-wine-color brocade, with ermine trim. It is worn over a red-velvet undergown. The fall of her headdress is black velvet, as is the band at the neckline of her gown and the edging on the undergown.

161. Katherine of Aragon, ca. 1510. Katherine of Aragon, Henry VIII's first wife and the mother of Mary Tudor, was a Spanish princess who established the fashions of her native land in the Tudor court. Her fitted gown is worn over a cone-shaped frame, or farthingale, and has fur-lined cone-shaped sleeves. Her chemise is seen at the square neckline of the gown and at the sleeves. She wears a jeweled gable coif with a black velvet veil hanging in back.

162. English ladies of the court, ca. 1528. Shown here are two ladies of the court, each one wearing a gable coif with split veils hanging in the back. The gowns with fitted bodices have bell-shaped gathered skirts and full fur-cuffed sleeves worn over false stuffed sleeves.

163. Italy, ca. 1530. This young woman's gown is burnt-orange velvet with gold embroidered trim. Her white chemise is puffed below the bodice. Her cap is made of both curled and flat gold ribbon.

164. Italian courtesans bleaching and styling their hair, ca. 1530. The seated woman wears a broad wooden brim with her hair pulled up and through it to keep the lye-based bleaching preparation from getting on her skin. She wears a shell-pink, soft linen chemise. The standing woman is arranging her frizzed blond hair. She wears a gown of wine-color velvet, trimmed in gold, over a white chemise.

165. France, ca. 1530. This lady wears a green satin gown with slashed puffs showing a lavender lining. The shoulders and caul of gold-color sheer fabric are embroidered and pearl studded. The girdle and the crown are gold color.

166. France, ca. 1530. This gentleman wears a blue gown slashed to show a dark-blue lining. His shirt, doublet, sleeves, trunk hose, and hose are white. The slashed shoes are blue. There is a gold embroidered band on the doublet and he wears a gold chain on his shoulders.

167. Henry VIII of England, ca. 1534. The square look of Henry VIII's fashions is exemplified by this broad-shouldered, padded and stuffed brocaded velvet gown with ermine-edged false sleeves. Under the puffed short sleeves of the gown are stuffed, tied-on jeweled sleeves. Under the gown he wears an embroidered satin jacket, or jerkin, with slashes and puffs on the bodice. The jerkin's skirt is arranged to reveal the elaborate codpiece. Henry preferred white silk stockings from Spain. His slashed lion's paw shoes are of white kid.

168. Anne Boleyn, ca. 1534. Anne Boleyn, Henry VIII's second wife and the mother of Elizabeth I, liked to wear bright colors. In her day, the false undersleeves and the underskirt were of the same material and color. Anne wore rose-colored sleeves and underskirt for her execution. Here she wears a white horseshoe-shaped hood or cap with a wired framework of pearls, fluted linen edging, and a black velvet fall.

169. Jane Seymour, ca. 1536. Jane Seymour, Henry VIII's third wife and the mother of Edward VI, wears a gold-and-jewel-decorated gable coif with the lappets pinned up and the black veil, or coronet, stiffened and pinned up. Her fitted gown is worn over a farthingale and is open in front, revealing a brocaded underskirt that matches the stuffed undersleeves. The cuffs of the oversleeves and edges of the skirt are covered by gold mesh.

170. Anne of Cleves, ca. 1539. Anne of Cleves was Henry's fourth wife. She brought the German touch to Tudor fashions. German fashions were generally more elaborate and fussier than those of the rest of Europe. Here, Anne wears a heavily jeweled velvet gown with puffed upper sleeves and giant set-in lower sleeves. Her jeweled coif features a sheer hood and lappets over a jeweled cap.

171. French court couple, ca. 1540. He wears a deep-blue gown with silver galloon and loops, and a white ermine collar. The doublet and codpiece are silver-gray satin with slashing showing the white shirt. His silver-gray trunk hose have white slashing; they

complement silver upper stocks and white hose. His dark-blue velvet cap has a white plume. The woman's bodice and petticoat are of white satin with gold embroidery. Her overskirt is gold-and-white brocade. The slashed sleeves are gold-color fabric with the white chemise sleeves bound with knotted gold ribbon. The same ribbon covers the white chemise at the shoulder. The white felt cap is decorated with pearls like those on the gown. She carries a white ostrich-tip fan. Her gloves, slashed shoes, and fan handle are red.

172. Italian courtesan, ca. 1540. This courtesan is showing her padded and slashed knickers. Most women of the period would not have worn any kind of pants, which were considered "male only" attire. Her rose-color gown has bands of trimming in gold-and-red brocade. Her stockings are white with red clocks (decorative figures); the chopines (a built-up platform shoe, designed to keep the wearer out of the mud or dirt of the streets) are white with red trim. She carries a flag-shaped fan.

173. Catherine Howard, ca. 1540. Henry VII's fifth wife was Catherine Howard. There is no authenticated portrait of her; this likeness is thought to be of her. Here Catherine wears a velvet gown with silk sleeves and underskirt. The collar and cuffs of her chemise are white. Her white coif has black velvet edging and a jeweled frame with a black fall.

174. Princess Elizabeth, ca. 1546. Princess Elizabeth, the daughter of Henry VIII and the ill-fated Anne Boleyn, became queen in 1558. As queen, she sent patterns to dressmakers in Europe to have gowns made; these foreign influences shaped English fashion of the times. Here she wears a court gown of taffeta with huge cone-shaped sleeves that fall to the back, over a brocaded skirt and undersleeves. She wears a jeweled cap with a shortened coronet of lace.

175. German royal children with their nanny, ca. 1550. The boy wears a dark-red velvet outfit trimmed with gold galloon. His black hat has gold-color ornaments and white feathers. He wears black shoes and white stockings. The girl wears a pink-velvet gown in the Spanish style, with gold trim, and a white apron and cap. Her doll is dressed in black and gold. The nanny is dressed in a black gown with a white apron, chemise, and cap. The embroidered trim on her blouse and apron is purple and green.

176. French courtiers wearing Spanish-style attire, ca. 1550. His cloak and cap are dark green, with gold embroidery. His doublet and trunk hose are pale-green silk, embroidered in gold and slashed to show white puffs. He wears white hose, gloves, and slippers, and has a white feather in his cap. The lady wears a gown of dark red with bands of silver embroidery, showing white puffs. Her ruff, wrist ruffles, and cap ruffle are white. Bands of pearls decorate her hair.

177. Upper-class French merchant and his wife, ca. 1550. She wears a mauve-and-gold brocaded gown with gold-and-plum trim. Her sleeves are bands of gold embroidery on a mauve ground. Her skirt is caught up and attached to the waist, revealing its plum-color velvet lining. Her petticoat is mauve, with gold embroidery and bands of gold and plum. Her cap is of plum velvet and has a sheer white fall. The collar and cuff ruffles were referred to as a "suit of ruffs." The man wears a deep-red velvet chamarre (robe). His puffed sleeves are decorated with pearl-studded gold bands. The gown is lined with black fur, which shows at the collar and the hem. His hose, shirt, and ruff, and the feather in his red-velvet cap, are white. His slashed shoe uppers also are of red velvet.

178. London merchant family, ca. 1550–1560. By the end of Henry VIII's reign, London's wealthy merchant class had begun to adopt many of the fashions of the nobility. Shown here are a London merchant and his wife and baby. He wears a brocaded silk houppelande with false hanging sleeves and fur trim, a starched ruff, and a velvet cap. Her gown has short, puffed, castellated sleeves. Her white linen cap is starched and wired. She wears a chain with a key and scissors. The baby, wrapped in a scarlet blanket, wears a pale brocaded gown and white ruff.

179. Prince Edward VI and attendant, ca. 1550. The fashions of the period of Edward VI (shown at right) changed little from those of his father, Henry VIII. Though to our eyes these styles appear quite elaborate, the trend was to less ostentation in decoration, notably a more modest use of jewelry.

180. Mary Tudor, ca. 1552. Princess Mary Tudor, in line for the English throne after Edward VI, wearing a Spanish-styled gown with high puffed sleeves over narrow lower sleeves. Her velvet gown is edged in ermine. Her cap has taken the form of a hat with a crown and is trimmed with pearls. The ruffs at the collar and sleeves are more modest in size than previously.

181. Mary Tudor and Philip of Spain, ca. 1554. Mary Tudor married Philip of Spain when she ascended the throne. She passed many sumptuary laws requiring her subjects to dress conservatively. Mary's own wardrobe remained splendid, but with muted colors. The bodice of this gown has "wings" at the shoulder to hide the ties of the oversleeves. She has a ruff and a stand-up lace collar; undersleeves decorated with lace trim, ribbons, and pearls; and a wired and jeweled cap.

182. Members of the Elizabethan court, ca. 1558–1560. The young lady and gentleman are representative of early Elizabethan court styles. She wears a wired stand-up lace ruff, a long bodice with padded sleeves, and a French farthingale (large pad or hoop worn at the waist) over a pleated taffeta skirt. He wears a peascod belly bodice, an odd style suggesting a potbelly or pregnancy. He also wears a codpiece, a style already on the wane; a soft, high-crowned hat; a starched ruff; and a fur-trimmed cape. Shoes were becoming narrower; the duckbill toe was by now passé.

183. Mary of Scotland and Lord Darnley, ca. 1566. Elizabeth's cousin, Mary of Scotland, claimed to be the proper heir to England's throne after Mary Tudor's death. Elizabeth, however, was made queen, and Mary was eventually beheaded for plotting against Elizabeth. Mary preferred the Spanish style of dress over that of the Elizabethan court. She is shown here with her husband, Lord Darnley, who had been a dandy and a suitor in Elizabeth's court.

184. Elizabethan lady and her husband, ca. 1580. Here is an Elizabethan lady at her toilet, shown wearing a floral embroidered silk chemise under her boned corset. She has a collared negligee of sheer fabric with a lace-edged collar. She holds an ivory comb. Her husband is wearing a linen nightshirt with a ruff set at collar and sleeve, a motif repeated in the ruffled trim. He also wears a linen nightcap, known as a biggin.

185. Elizabeth I of England, ca. 1588. Elizabeth I set the style for her era, possibly one of the most artificial-appearing eras in fashion history. Here, her satin gown is jeweled from top to bottom, with padded, stuffed sleeves and false sleeves. The drum farthingale has a train falling in back; double strands of pearls drape the neckline and bodice. She wears a stand-up "Tudor ruff"; a wired, jeweled sheer train rises above her head. Her crimped and dyed wig, combed over a wire frame, is decorated with ropes of pearl.

186. Two London ladies of high rank, ca. 1590. The lady on the left is dressed in day attire—a satin gown worn over a brocaded petticoat. The gown's short puffed sleeves, decorated with ribbon and jeweled pins, are worn over padded undersleeves. Completing the costume are a tasseled scarf, ruffs, and a plumed high hat. At the right is a noblewoman dressed to attend church. Over her gown she wears a mantle wired to stand up above the shoulders. Her lace-trimmed cap, wired into shape, was known as the "Mary Stuart"; it has a sheer fall.

187. English sailor and farmer, ca. 1600. A sailor (left) and farmer (right) in conversation. English naval officers wore their own clothes, but mariners were issued outfits consisting of canvas knee-length breeches, strong knitted wool hose, and a canvas shirt. The loose tunic reached just below the waist. On land, the sailor wore black leather shoes; he usually went barefoot aboard ship. For shore he wore a ruff and felt hat. The farmer is dressed for town in a jerkin with false sleeves worn over a doublet and trunk hose. He wears a neck ruff and a felt hat.

188. English nobleman and lady, ca. 1600. Here, an English nobleman greets a lady. She wears padded brocade undersleeves. The undersleeves can be glimpsed through her long velvet false sleeves, which match the full skirt worn over a modified farthingale known as a bum roll, a pad worn around the waist to support and shape the skirt. The gentleman wears a peascod belly doublet, padded sleeves, and elaborately embroidered paned trunk hose. (Panes were stiffened fabric strips.) His stockings are decorated with embroidery. The lady wears a cartwheel ruff; the gentleman wears the stiffened, embroidered "Tudor ruff."

189. Women's headgear and hairstyles, 1400–1450. a. Italy, ca. 1400. **b–c.** England, ca. 1400. **d–e.** Germany, ca. 1410. **f.** Italy, ca. 1410. **g.** Italy, ca. 1420. **h.** Germany, ca. 1430. **i–j.** Italy, ca. 1430. **k.** Germany, ca. 1440. **l.** France, ca. 1440. **m.** Italy, ca. 1440. **n.** France, ca. 1450. **o.** Italy, ca. 1450. **p.** Italy, ca. 1450. **q.** England, ca. 1450.

190. Men's headgear and hairstyles, 1400–1450. a–k. Ca. 1400–1450. **l–m.** Ca. 1450.

191. Men's headgear and hairstyles, 1450–1490. a. England, ca. 1450. **b.** France, ca. 1450. **c.** Italy, ca. 1450. **d.** Italy, ca. 1460. **e.** England, ca. 1460. **f–g.** Italy, ca. 1480. **h–i.** France, ca. 1480. **j.** Hairstyle, ca. 1400. **k.** France, ca. 1480. **l.** Germany, ca. 1490. **m–n.** France, ca. 1490.

192. Men's headgear and hairstyles, 1500–1550. a–c. France, ca. 1500. **b.** Switzerland, ca. 1520. **d.** Italy, ca. 1520. **e–f.** Germany, ca. 1520. **g.** France, ca. 1530. **h.** Spain, ca. 1540. **i–j.** Germany, ca. 1530. **k–l.** France, ca. 1545. **m.** England, ca. 1540. **n.** Spain, ca. 1550.

193. Women's headgear and hairstyles, 1450–1500. a. Italy, ca. 1450. **b.** France, ca. 1450. **c–d.** France, ca. 1460. **e.** Germany, ca. 1470. **f.** Spain, ca. 1470. **g.** Germany, ca. 1470. **h.** France, ca. 1470. **i.** Italy, ca. 1490. **j–k.** France, ca. 1480. **l–m.** Italy, ca. 1490. **n.** Italy, ca. 1490. **o–p.** Italy, ca. 1500. **q.** Italy, ca. 1500. **r–s.** France, ca. 1500.

194. Hats, shoes, and accessories, 1490–1640. a. Ca. 1490. **b.** Ca. 1510. **c.** Ca. 1490. **d–e.** Ca. 1520. **f.** Ca. 1510. **g.** Ca. 1520. **h.** Ca. 1525. **i.** Ca. 1516. **j.** Ca. 1640. **k.** Ca.1540. **l.** Ca. 1520. **m.** Ca. 1530. **n.** Ca. 1535. **o.** Ca. 1500. **p.** Ca. 1540. **q.** Ca. 1550. **r–s.** Ca. 1540. **t.** Ca. 1510. **u.** Ca. 1520. **v.** Ca. 1500. **w.** Ca. 1540. **x.** Ca. 1550. **y.** Ca. 1510. **z.** Ca. 1500. **aa.** Ca. 1510. **bb.** Ca. 1520. **cc.** Ca. 1515. Ca. 1540. **dd.** Ca. 1525.

195. Hats, shoes, and accessories, 1500–1600. a–d. Ca. 1550. **e.** Ca. 1555. **f–g.** Ca. 1560. **h–i.** Ca. 1555. **j.** Ca. 1575. **k.** Ca. 1580. **l.** Ca. 1570. **m–n.** Ca. 1575. **o.** Ca. 1590. **p.** Ca. 1500–1600. **q.** Ca. 1590. **r.** Ca. 1550. **s.** Ca. 1575. **t.** Ca. 1580. **u.** Ca. 1590. **v.** Ca. 1570. **w.** Ca. 1560. **x–y.** Ca. 1590. **z.** Ca. 1560.

196. Women's headgear and hairstyles, 1500–1550.

197. Greek and Roman footwear.

198. Byzantine footwear.

199. Medieval footwear. a. Soft leather boot with jewels, 10th c. **b.** Low-topped button-on shoe with padded "scorpion" toe, 12th c. **c.** Soft, low leather tie-on shoe, 13th c. **d.** Soft, low, leather shoe with embroidery and pearls, 11th c. **e.** Soft leather boot with sewn-on sole, 11th c. **f.** Patten (a thick sole of wood, attached to a shoe by leather straps) worn outside to protect poulaine-styled shoes, 14th c. **g.** Low-topped shoe with straps and pointed, padded toe, 14th c. **h.** Wooden patten with modified heel, 15th c. **i.** Poulaine-style shoe on a patten with padded toe, dagged trim and fur at the ankle, 14th c. **j.** Shoe and wooden patten, 15th c. **k.** Man's boot, 15th c. **l.** Lady's chopine, 15th c.

200. Renaissance footwear and accessories. a–e. Early 1400s. **f–k.** 1400s. **l–m.** Early 1500s. **n.** 1500s. **o.** Early 1500s. **p.** 1500s. **q.** 1400s–1500s. **r.** Early 1500s. **s–t.** 1500s. **u–v.** Early 1500s. **w–z.** 1500s.